DATE DUE

MR 3			
JE 10 02			

DEMCO 38-296

**The
Reagan
Reversal**

R

The Reagan Reversal

Foreign Policy and the
End of the Cold War

Beth A. Fischer

University of Missouri Press
Columbia and London

Copyright © 1997 by
The Curators of the University of Missouri
University of Missouri Press, Columbia, Missouri 65201
Printed and bound in the United States of America
All rights reserved
5 4 3 2 1   01 00 99 98 97

Library of Congress Cataloging-in-Publication Data

Fischer, Beth A., 1964–
    The Reagan reversal : foreign policy and the end of the Cold War /
    Beth A. Fischer.
        p. cm.
    Includes bibliographical references and index.
    ISBN 0-8262-1138-0 (alk. paper)
    1. United States—Foreign relations—Soviet Union. 2. Soviet
Union—Foreign relations—United States. 3. United States—Foreign
relations—1981–1989. 4. Reagan, Ronald. I. Title.
E876.F569 1997
327.73047—dc21   97-30459
                                                                 CIP

∞ ™ This paper meets the requirements of the
American National Standard for Permanence of Paper
for Printed Library Materials, Z39.48, 1984.

Designer: Stephanie Foley
Typesetter: BOOKCOMP
Printer and binder: Thomson-Shore, Inc.
Typeface: Berkeley

To Gerard

Contents

Preface

THIS IS NOT THE BOOK I set out to write. While sifting through foreign policy documents for another project, I became intrigued by what appeared to have been an abrupt and dramatic reversal in the Reagan administration's approach to the Soviet Union in early 1984. In January of that year President Reagan abandoned his hard-line approach to Moscow and began pursuing a more congenial relationship between the superpowers. Since this policy reversal preceded Mikhail Gorbachev and drastic reforms within the Soviet Union, I was curious as to why the Reagan administration would have suddenly reversed course. My hunch was that Secretary of State George Shultz had brought about the change. Shultz was a relative newcomer to the administration at that point, and was more moderate than his colleagues. I suspected that Shultz had somehow managed to redirect U.S. Soviet policy in a direction more to his liking. I had thought that I would be writing a book about a powerful secretary of state.

But I could find no evidence to support my working hypothesis. The more digging I did, the more my research led me away from the secretary. Frustrated and more puzzled than ever, I was forced to reexamine my assumptions about the Reagan administration's way of formulating foreign policy. Like many others, I had assumed that the president played an inconsequential role in foreign policy development. I had assumed that Reagan was simply the administration's spokesperson. His role was merely to read the policy statements that others prepared for him. It was only when I began to reconsider this assumption that the answer to my puzzle began to unfold. As I reread documents and speeches it became increasingly clear that Reagan's fingerprints were all over them. Much to my surprise, I would be writing a book about a widely misunderstood president, one who was far more involved in foreign policy making than contemporary scholars had believed.

Much of the evidence for this book comes from interviews. I am deeply indebted to National Security Advisor Robert McFarlane, Secretary of Defense Caspar Weinberger, and Ambassador to the Soviet Union Jack Matlock. All three were generous with their time and provided me with invaluable information. A host of other government officials, all of whom prefer to remain anonymous, also provided valuable insights into the workings of the Reagan administration and the pivotal events in the fall of 1983.

Three faculty members at the University of Toronto deserve special mention. Jean Edward Smith read through various drafts of the manuscript and was absolutely unmerciful in his criticism of my writing style. I thank him for that. Janice Gross Stein challenged my arguments, pressing me to think more critically. While Smith demanded that I write better, and Stein demanded that I think more rigorously, David Welch helped me to cope with all these demands. His enthusiasm, compassion, and insight were crucial to the completion of the manuscript.

This book has benefited tremendously from the help of others. I am grateful to Ole Holsti, Ned Lebow, Yaacov Vertzberger, and several anonymous reviewers for taking time out of their busy schedules to read the manuscript. Their constructive criticism has greatly improved the quality of the book. The Director and Editor-in-Chief of the University of Missouri Press, Beverly Jarrett, also deserves special thanks for overseeing this project and moving it along so quickly. The generous funding of the Social Sciences and Humanities Research Council of Canada was also pivotal.

I owe a special thanks to the Fischer family—Ruth, Bruce, Gwen, and Lynn. They weren't always sure as to what I was doing, but they were supportive nonetheless. My family also instilled in me a quality that is crucial to any writer—a sense of humor. The ability to chuckle over the oddities of academia acted as a life preserver during the stormier days of writing this book.

And finally, words simply cannot express my gratitude to my husband, Gerard Waslen. I have always maintained that the spouses of doctoral students deserve some special recognition. Sainthood seems most appropriate. Although busy with his own career, Gerard took the time to read through each and every draft of this book. Consequently, he now knows far more about U.S. foreign policy than he ever cared to. His endless patience, enthusiastic support, and sympathetic ear have been both a sense of comfort and an inspiration. The publication of this book is just as much his triumph as it is mine.

The
Reagan
Reversal

Introduction

THE INTERNATIONAL POLITICAL SYSTEM is now in the throes of a major transformation. The collapse of the Soviet Union and the ending of the cold war have profoundly changed the international political arena. The bipolar arrangement that structured international relations for nearly forty years has collapsed, and it remains unclear what type of system will replace it. This transformation began during the Reagan presidency. It was during the mid-1980s that U.S.-Soviet relations shifted from cold war antagonism toward rapprochement.

The conventional view is that the United States played a reactive role in bringing the cold war to an end. Washington simply responded to the momentous changes that were taking place within the Soviet Union. When Mikhail Gorbachev became leader of the USSR in 1985, the Kremlin became more conciliatory toward Washington. In response, the Reagan administration abandoned its hard-line posture toward Moscow. According to this view, Gorbachev's "new thinking" and congenial personality led the Reagan administration to seek a rapprochement. Washington simply followed Moscow's lead. For example, in his classic work *American Foreign Policy since World War II*, John Spanier contends that Gorbachev faced a domestic crisis upon taking office. The Soviet economy was nearing a complete breakdown, and apathy and lack of discipline in the workplace were keeping productivity low. Gorbachev had little choice: Soviet resources had to be devoted to domestic rebuilding rather than to fostering a strong global presence. The Soviet Union could no longer afford to maintain its sphere of influence, or to compete in an expensive arms race. Consequently, Gorbachev was forced to seek a rapprochement with the United States. According to Spanier, the Reagan administration

1

merely responded to Gorbachev's new conciliatory posture. Alexander George supports Spanier's assessment. George writes, "The . . . milieu of East-West relations profoundly changed . . . largely because Mikhail Gorbachev changed the 'reality' of East-West relations by setting into motion fundamental reforms in the domestic structure of the Soviet Union and by introducing a radical reconceptualization of the Soviet approach to international relations."[1]

Indeed, both liberals and conservatives have an interest in perpetuating the notion that Washington changed its Soviet policy only after Moscow had begun to reform.[2] Ideological liberals had been critical of the Reagan administration's initial hard-line policy and military buildup, fearing that such policies raised the probability of a superpower war. Many also questioned the president's intellectual prowess. Already critical of Reagan's Soviet policy, liberals are therefore inclined to accept the view that Gorbachev led the president on the path to ending the cold war. A lucky bumbler, Reagan was simply in the right place at the right time.

Conservatives, on the other hand, also have reason to support the idea that Reagan responded to changes in Soviet policy. In this view, the administration's original hard-line rhetoric and military buildup forced the Soviet Union to its knees. Gorbachev had to seek a rapprochement with Washington because his country could no longer compete with the United States. By standing firm, President Reagan had forced the Kremlin to capitulate in the cold war. Moscow succumbed, and democracy proved victorious.

This book challenges the conventional wisdom regarding the Reagan administration's role in ending the cold war. It contends that Washington did not merely respond to changes within the Soviet Union. In fact, the Reagan administration began seeking a rapprochement with the Kremlin *before* the Soviets began to reform. The White House switched to a more conciliatory policy toward Moscow in

1. John Spanier, *American Foreign Policy since World War II*, 347–50; Alexander L. George, "The Transition in U.S.-Soviet Relations, 1985–1990: An Interpretation from the Perspective of International Relations Theory and Political Psychology," 471.

2. For a review of competing explanations of the cold war's demise, see Charles W. Kegley Jr., "How Did the Cold War Die: Principles for an Autopsy."

January 1984—fifteen months before Gorbachev became leader of the Soviet Union, and more than two years before the introduction of *glasnost* and *perestroika*.

As will be detailed, the Reagan administration's stated policy toward Moscow was especially hard-line through October 1983. On October 31 Deputy Secretary of State Kenneth Dam delivered a speech on superpower relations that epitomized the administration's early position toward Moscow. Dam contended that East and West were engaged in a zero-sum competition for spheres of influence. The Soviet Union posed the most immediate threat to U.S. security, he argued, as was evidenced by their massive military buildup and the manner in which they "intervened" militarily throughout the globe. Dam declared that the primary aim of U.S. policy was to thwart Soviet expansionism, and that Washington would continue to take a hard-line approach as long as the Soviets continued their "quest for absolute security." He also warned that superpower relations were not likely to improve in the near future. "We are now in a period of uncertainty as to the immediate future of U.S.-Soviet relations," he cautioned. "We should be wary of illusions about the possibility of quick or dramatic breakthroughs."[3]

Only ten weeks later, however, Washington reversed course. On January 16, 1984, President Reagan delivered an address on superpower relations that proved to be the turning point in his administration's approach to the Kremlin. With this speech, Reagan began seeking a rapprochement. The president expressed a more nuanced understanding of the superpower relationship, and introduced new policy goals and strategies. In sharp contrast to Dam's remarks two months earlier, he played down the ideological differences between the two capitals, and spoke at length about the superpowers' "common interests." Foremost among these interests, he asserted, was the desire for peace. Reagan warned of the dangers of war, and declared that the United States posed no threat to the security of the Soviet Union. The president also spoke of the urgent need to address "dangerous misunderstandings" between the two capitals. Toward this end he

3. Kenneth W. Dam, "Challenges of U.S.-Soviet Relations at the 50-Year Mark," October 31, 1983, *Department of State Bulletin [DSB]* (December 1983), 27.

called for the immediate institutionalization of high-level dialogue, new efforts in arms reduction, and the implementation of a wide range of confidence-building measures. The aim of U.S. policy was now to facilitate "cooperation and understanding" between the superpowers.[4]

President Reagan's January 16 address was not simply an aberration. Rather, it was a turning point. Throughout 1984 and 1985 others within the administration echoed Reagan's call for "cooperation and understanding" between the superpowers, and underscored that Washington "posed no threat" to Soviet security. The superpowers had a common interest in avoiding war and "misunderstandings," they reiterated. Likewise, Reagan officials continued to speak of the "imperative" need for superpower dialogue.

The policy changes that Reagan introduced in 1984 are striking for a number of reasons. Most importantly, they are remarkable because they were implemented before the Soviets began to reform. In January 1984 Yuri Andropov was general secretary of the USSR, and there was no indication that Moscow intended to introduce radical changes to its foreign policy. The old guard within the Kremlin was still fighting the cold war. The conventional view that Washington responded to changes within the Soviet Union is therefore inaccurate.

The degree to which the administration altered its stated policy toward Moscow is also striking. This was not simply a case of "fine-tuning." Both policy goals and strategies changed in 1984. In many respects, these changes represented a wholesale reversal of the administration's earlier policies. The Reagan administration had been the most vehemently anticommunist administration in U.S. history. The president himself had been denouncing communists for over forty years, since he had been an actor in Hollywood. He had repeatedly asserted that democracies must do all they can to undermine communism and to stop its spread. It is remarkable, therefore, that Reagan would suddenly begin speaking of "common interests" and the need to join together to solve global problems.

The speed with which the Reagan administration switched course is also extraordinary. On October 31, 1983, Deputy Secretary Dam struck a hard-line posture toward the Soviets, and suggested that

---

4. Reagan, "The U.S.-Soviet Relationship," January 16, 1984, *American Foreign Policy: Current Documents [AFP:CD] 1984*, 406–11.

superpower relations would not improve in the near future. On January 16, 1984, the president began seeking a rapprochement with the Kremlin. The Reagan administration reversed course within a mere ten weeks.

Finally, the Reagan administration not only changed its stated policy, but it significantly revised its image of the Kremlin and its understanding of the nature of the superpower relationship. Such revisions are highly unusual. For example, before 1984 official policy statements exhibited a Manichaean understanding of superpower relations: Moscow and Washington were engaged in a zero-sum competition for spheres of influence. The Soviets were the enemy. There was no common ground. However, beginning in 1984, the administration's policy statements revealed a more complex image of the Kremlin and a more nuanced understanding of superpower relations. While Soviets and Americans had ideological differences, they also had many common interests. This change in the administration's view is curious because psychological studies have repeatedly shown that fundamental beliefs about others tend not to change. Moreover, images of one's enemy tend to be especially entrenched. It is striking, therefore, that the Reagan administration would revise its image of the Kremlin.[5]

The primary aim of this book, then, is to determine why the Reagan administration so abruptly reversed course in January 1984. If Washington was not simply responding to Soviet overtures, then what caused the changes in U.S. Soviet policy?

---

5. On the rigidity of images of others, see Alexander L. George, *Presidential Decisionmaking in Foreign Policy: The Effective Use of Information and Advice*, 68–70; Robert Jervis, *Perception and Misperception in International Politics;* Herbert C. Kelman, *International Behavior;* and Keith L. Shimko, *Images and Arms Control: Perceptions of the Soviet Union in the Reagan Administration*, especially 11–26. On enemy images, see Ole Holsti, "Cognitive Dynamics and Images of the Enemy"; Brett Silverstein and Catherine Flamenbaum, "Biases in the Perception and Cognition of the Actions of Enemies"; Brett Silverstein, "Enemy Images: The Psychology of U.S. Attitudes and Cognitions Regarding the Soviet Union"; D. J. Finlay, O. R. Holsti, and R. R. Fagen, *Enemies in Politics;* Mark Snyder, Elizabeth D. Tanke, and Ellen Berscheid, "Social Perception and Interpersonal Behavior: On the Self-Fulfilling Nature of Social Stereotypes"; Renee Weber and Jennifer Crocker, "Cognitive Processes in the Revision of Stereotypic Beliefs"; Yaacov I. Vertzberger, *The World in Their Minds: Information Processing, Cognition, and Perception in Foreign Policy Decision Making*, 118–27; and Jervis, *Perception and Misperception*, especially 310–15.

Although the literature on U.S. foreign policy is vast, there has been comparatively little theoretical work regarding change in such policy. Much of the literature focuses either on the policy-making process, or on the substance of American foreign policy. Both types of studies tend to ignore the issue of change. For example, policy-making studies typically focus on how different actors, such as interest groups and bureaucratic organizations, seek to influence policy outcomes. Such studies focus on factors that constrain policy change, rather than on factors that may facilitate or catalyze a change in policy.[6]

Likewise, studies that have focused on the substance of U.S. foreign policy have also ignored the issue of change. This is no doubt due in part to the relative stability of U.S. policy throughout the cold war. For four decades Washington divided the globe into spheres of influence and sought to contain communism. The struggle between communism and democracy defined not only Washington's position toward the East, but also its relations with Europe, Asia, and the Third World. Because U.S. foreign policy was relatively stable, scholars focused on issues related to stability.

The demise of the cold war has brought an end to this period of relative stability. The United States has been forced to adjust to the emerging world order, as has every other nation. Each has had to reassess its role in the international arena, its relationship to other nations, and the structure and purpose of existing international organizations. Foreign policy change is becoming more prevalent. Therefore, it is imperative that it be studied more closely. As Charles F. Hermann has observed, "We are on the dividing line between epochs. Under these circumstances it is not enough for those engaged in . . . foreign policy studies to examine regularities and patterns of association under assumed conditions of *ceteris paribus*. We need a much more vigorous effort to characterize the conditions that can produce decisions for

---

6. On foreign policy change, see Kal J. Holsti, *Why Nations Realign;* Kjell Goldman, *Change and Stability in Foreign Policy: The Problems and Possibilities of Détente;* Charles F. Hermann, "Changing Course: When Governments Choose to Redirect Foreign Policy"; and Jerel Rosati, Joe D. Hagan, and Martin W. Sampson III, *Foreign Policy Restructuring: How Governments Respond to Global Change.*

dramatic redirection in foreign policy."[7] In short, there is a need to consider foreign policy change more systematically.

There are two broad types of foreign policy change. On the one hand, there are cases in which foreign policy changes because a new government or a new leader has come to power. The new government's vision of foreign policy differs from its predecessor's, and it therefore implements policies which differ from those of the previous government. The second broad type of foreign policy change occurs when an existing government chooses to change course. In these cases, a catalyst of some sort causes the government to reassess its standing policy, and to move in a new direction. Hermann calls such instances cases of "self-correcting change—when the current actors change their course in foreign policy."[8]

Scholars have posited four main sources of self-correcting policy change.[9] In the first instance, *changes in the international environment* may cause governments to revise their foreign policies. For example, the rise or fall of great powers, the outbreak of war or peace, the creation or dissolution of alliance systems, and other factors may cause a state to change its foreign policy. Structural realists argue that "governments respond in a rational (or at least, reasonable) manner to the reward and punishment contingencies of the international environment." If these reward and punishment contingencies shift, so too does a government's foreign policy. Kenneth Waltz has argued more specifically that in an anarchic, bipolar world, the international distribution of capabilities is the primary determinant of a state's behavior. If this distribution changes, then so will a state's approach to international affairs. As Janice Gross Stein has succinctly put it, "Rational states recognize structural change, reorder their interests, adjust their policies to maximize their interests, and adapt."[10] A government that fails to adapt, risks its survival.

7. Hermann, "Changing Course," 20.

8. Ibid., 5.

9. Ibid.; see also Janice Gross Stein, "Ideas, Even Good Ideas, Are Not Enough: Changing Canada's Foreign and Defense Policies."

10. Philip Tetlock, "Learning in U.S. and Soviet Foreign Policy: In Search of an Elusive Concept," 24; Kenneth N. Waltz, *Theory of International Politics;* Stein, "Ideas," 41.

Foreign policy might also change in response to *domestic politics*. In democratic societies, shifts in public opinion can put pressure on a government to revise its approach to foreign relations. An administration might be especially sensitive to changes in public attitudes during an election year. Failing to respond to constituents' views during such a time might conceivably lead to a government's fall from power.[11]

Hermann also points out that *"bureaucratic advocacy"* might cause a government to redirect its foreign policy. In such cases a group or faction within the government becomes an advocate of change. The members of this group may be located in one agency, or they may be scattered among different organizations. Regardless, they have some means for regular interaction. In order to be effective, these advocates have to be in a position to determine policy outcomes, or have access to those who have such authority.[12]

Finally, foreign policy change may be *leader-driven*. In such cases "change results from the determined efforts of an authoritative policy maker, frequently the head of government, who imposes his own vision of the basic redirection necessary in foreign policy. The leader must have the conviction, power, and energy to compel his government to change course."[13] If a leader has the authority to direct foreign policy making, then a change in his or her views could lead to a change in official policy. Cognitive psychology focuses on questions pertaining to decision making and learning, and thus can be especially useful in understanding a leader's changing views. "Psychologists remind us that policy makers react not to the international environment as such, but rather to their mental representations of that environment," Philip E. Tetlock has rightly noted. "To understand

---

11. See Ole R. Holsti, "Public Opinion and Foreign Policy: Challenges to the Almond-Lippmann Consensus"; Benjamin I. Page and Robert Y. Shapiro, *The Rational Public: Fifty Years of Trends in Americans' Policy Preferences;* Thomas Risse-Kappen, "Public Opinion, Domestic Structure, and Foreign Policy in Liberal Democracies"; Miroslav Nincic, "The United States, the Soviet Union, and the Politics of Opposites"; and David Cortright, *Peace Works: The Citizen's Role in Ending the Cold War.*

12. Hermann, "Changing Course," 11–12.

13. Ibid., 11.

the evolution of policy we need to understand our cognitive biases and limitations: our tendencies to oversimplify complex problems, to be oblivious to trade-offs, and to assimilate new evidence into our preconceptions."[14]

As already noted, individuals do not change their views easily. Former secretary of state Henry Kissinger argued that political leaders are particularly disinclined to change their minds. "It is an illusion to believe that leaders gain in profundity while they gain experience," he has written. "The convictions that leaders have formed before reaching high office are the intellectual capital they will consume as long as they continue in office."[15] Nevertheless, there has been a burgeoning literature on the relationship between "learning" and foreign policy making. In his pioneering studies during the early 1980s, Lloyd Etheredge was one of the first to introduce the concept of learning into studies of policy making. Etheredge drew upon various sources in psychology and organizational studies in an effort to define learning in a way that could be useful for political scientists. Subsequent work on learning has, for the most part, fallen into two categories. On the one hand, some scholars have focused upon defining "learning" in a more explicit manner. For example, in their volume, *Learning in U.S. and Soviet Foreign Policy,* Breslauer and Tetlock and colleagues consider in detail the relationship between leaders' changing beliefs and their nations' foreign policies. The authors' aim is to refine the concept of learning. Consequently, they employ a learning theory approach in a variety of cases in an effort to categorize different types of learning, and to address some of its theoretical and normative difficulties. On the other hand, some scholars have employed a learning approach in order to better understand specific cases of foreign policy change. For example, Sarah E. Mendelson has considered whether learning can explain the Soviet decision to withdraw from Afghanistan. Likewise, Stein has used the concept of learning to offer fresh insight into Mikhail Gorbachev's "new thinking" on security, and how such thinking came to be official policy. The underlying concern of all these

14. Tetlock, "Learning in U.S. and Soviet Foreign Policy," 54.
15. Henry Kissinger, *White House Years,* 54.

studies, however, is the relationship between leaders' changing views and self-correcting policy change.[16]

This book focuses on one case of self-correcting policy change, and thus will prove useful in better understanding such kinds of change. Drawing upon the theoretical work cited above, the book will compare four competing explanations of the change in the Reagan administration's stated policy toward the Soviet Union. The aim is to determine which is most fully explanatory.

When seeking to explain a case of policy change one must be explicit at the outset about what needs to be explained. This study contends that any explanation of a policy shift, be it foreign or domestic policy, must address three aspects of that shift:

1. The explanation must clearly state the *catalyst* for the policy shift. It should explain what, exactly, caused the government to reconsider its standing policy. For example, an event, a person, an idea, or a technological development might cause a government to reassess its approach to foreign relations.

2. The explanation must explain the *timing* of the policy change. In order to be satisfactory, an explanation of policy change must explain why the policy shifted at the time it did, as opposed to some other point in time. In this case, an explanation must demonstrate why U.S. policy changed in January 1984, as opposed to January 1981, when Reagan took office, or March 1985, when Gorbachev came to power, or some other date. Just as importantly, the explanation must spell out why the administration reversed course within a mere ten weeks.

3. Finally, an explanation of the policy change must explain *the nature of the policy changes*. It should make clear why policy changed in the manner it did. The policy-making process is

16. Lloyd Etheredge, "Government Learning: An Overview"; Lloyd Etheredge, *Can Governments Learn?*; George W. Breslauer and Philip E. Tetlock, eds., *Learning in U.S. and Soviet Foreign Policy,* especially 3–100 and 825–56; Sarah E. Mendelson, "Internal Battles and External Wars: Politics, Learning, and the Soviet Withdrawal from Afghanistan"; and Janice Gross Stein, "Cognitive Psychology and Political Learning: Gorbachev as an Uncommitted Thinker and Motivated Learner." See also Jack S. Levy, "Learning and Foreign Policy: Sweeping a Conceptual Minefield."

extraordinarily complex, as is the speech-writing process. Many officials, meetings, and discussions are involved. In the case of Reagan's turning-point address, numerous drafts of the speech were circulated around the executive branch before there was agreement on the final document. The point is, policy statements are carefully crafted documents. New themes are introduced for a reason, after much consideration. In order to be fully explanatory then, an explanation must spell out (a) what the new themes mean, and (b) why these themes were introduced. In this case, an explanation should spell out not only why the Reagan administration became more conciliatory, but also why it began speaking of "dangerous misunderstandings" between the superpowers, the "imperative" need for dialogue, and why officials began asserting the United States "posed no threat to the security of the Soviet Union."

Oftentimes, studies of policy change focus on only one of these three factors, assuming, for example, that it is enough to explain only the timing of the policy change. This study seeks to be more comprehensive. In order to be fully explanatory, an explanation of the change in the Reagan administration's Soviet policy must explain all three aspects of the policy shift. Each of the competing explanations will therefore be assessed in terms of the three criteria set out above. The most satisfactory explanation will spell out what caused the administration to rethink its standing policy, why the policy changed between October 31, 1983, and January 16, 1984, and why certain themes came to dominate Washington's new approach to Moscow.

For example, let us examine how a structural realist explanation of the policy change would fare in terms of these three criteria. As noted, structural realists argue that shifts in the international distribution of capabilities cause nations to change their behavior in the international arena. In this case, structural realists would argue that a shift in the military balance of power caused Washington to seek a rapprochement with Moscow. Such an explanation of the policy change is unsatisfactory, as is demonstrated by testing it against the three criteria. In the first instance, the catalyst for the policy change is underspecified. The realist explanation posits that shifts in relative capabilities caused the policy change. However, Soviet and American relative capabilities had shifted before without any changes in the basically antagonistic superpower relationship. Immediately after World War Two the United States was both militarily and economically stronger than the war-torn USSR. Bilateral relations were tense and became more acrimonious as the 1950s and the cold war set in. By the 1970s the Soviet Union had attained a rough military parity with the United States, as was acknowledged in the first Strategic Arms Limitation Treaty (SALT I). Despite this, relations remained rancorous. And in the early 1980s relations continued to be hostile despite the argument of some that the United States had become militarily weaker than the USSR. In short, superpower relations had remained antagonistic for four decades despite shifts in relative military capabilities. The structural realist explanation fails to specify exactly what caused the Reagan administration to reverse course.

Structural realism also does not explain the timing of the policy change. It simply posits that a state's behavior will change in response to a shift in the international distribution of capabilities. It does not specify how soon after such a shift a policy change will occur. Moreover, not only does structural realism fail to explain why U.S. policy reversed course in January 1984, it fails to explain why it changed course within a span of ten weeks.

Finally, structural realism cannot explain the nature of the policy changes. It simply predicts that a shift in relative capabilities will yield a change in states' international behavior. It does not specify whether the policy will shift in the direction of conciliation or in the direction of belligerence. In this case, either scenario is conceivable. For example, if the Soviets had developed military superiority, Washington might have decided to switch to a more conciliatory posture, in the hope that better relations would prompt Moscow to agree to arms reduction. On the other hand, Washington might have taken an even more aggressive position, directing even greater resources to the military, in the belief that the United States faced an even more dire threat. Structural realism, then, predicts both policy outcomes. And a theory that predicts everything, explains nothing. Moreover, not only does the theory fail to predict the general direction of the policy change, it cannot explain the specific themes that came to dominate U.S. policy, such as the references to "dangerous misunderstandings," and assurances that Washington "posed no threat" to Soviet security.

There is no doubt that relative economic and military capabilities have played a role in Soviet-American relations. The decades-long arms race and the creation of global alliance systems attest to this. However, these factors alone cannot explain why the United States moved from a confrontational approach to the Soviet Union to a more conciliatory one in January 1984. Structural realism fails to explain the exact catalyst for the policy change, the timing of the shift, and the nature of the policy changes.

The bulk of this book will compare in detail three other possible explanations for the change in the Reagan administration's Soviet policy. Chapter 3 will consider the possibility that domestic politics forced the Reagan administration to abruptly change course. Perhaps the White House was responding to shifts in public opinion. Nineteen eighty-four was a presidential election year, and it has been argued that foreign policy was the president's Achilles' heel during his second election campaign. Some analysts have maintained that Reagan's hard-line approach to Moscow had caused concern among moderate voters. In this view, the American public had grown increasingly fearful that the president would entangle the United States in a war. Chapter 3 will consider the possibility that the administration switched to a more conciliatory approach to the USSR in order to appeal to these moderate voters.

Chapter 4 examines a bureaucratic politics explanation. It considers the possibility that personnel changes within the administration brought about the shift in U.S. Soviet policy. George Shultz became secretary of state in 1982, and Robert McFarlane took over as national security adviser in October 1983. Both men were more moderate than their predecessors, and favored a more forthcoming approach to Moscow. Chapter 4 considers whether Shultz and McFarlane could have acted as advocates of change, and redirected U.S. policy according to their own views.

Chapter 5 considers the possibility of leader-driven policy change. As noted, when a leader has the authority to direct foreign policy, a change in that leader's personal views can lead to a change in official policy. In the United States, the president has such authority. Although the Constitution divides power over the conduct of foreign relations between Congress and the executive, tradition and legal precedent have established the president as the preeminent authority in the making of foreign policy.[17] In the United States, therefore, a change in a president's personal views can lead to a change in U.S. foreign policy. Chapter 5 considers whether a shift in President Reagan's views brought about the reversal in U.S. Soviet policy.

Before comparing these competing explanations in greater detail, it is necessary to clarify the manner in which U.S. Soviet policy changed in January 1984. Therefore, the following chapter will focus on the Reagan administration's stated policy toward Moscow between 1981 and 1985. Its aim is to establish that the administration did in fact reverse course between October 31, 1983, and January 16, 1984. The chapter will also demonstrate that not only did policy goals and strategies change, but so, too, did fundamental assumptions about the Kremlin and superpower relations.

Some final words of caution must be added. This book is primarily concerned with the Reagan administration's *stated* policy toward the Soviet Union. References to the "administration's approach," "the administration's view," and the like refer to official policy statements, as recorded in *The Weekly Compilation of Presidential Documents, The Department of State Bulletin,* and *American Foreign Policy: Current Documents.* Such references are not intended to suggest that all members of the Reagan administration personally agreed with these official policy statements. Indeed, within the administration there were deep personal differences regarding Soviet policy, and these disputes will be detailed in Chapter 4.

Moreover, the book's principal aim is to determine why the Reagan administration reversed course in January 1984. It seeks to explain why Washington abandoned its hard-line approach to Moscow and began seeking a rapprochement. The book will therefore focus primarily on the period before the change occurred; that is, the first

17. See *United States v Curtiss-Wright Export Corporation,* 299 US 304 (1936); John Tower, Edmund Muskie, and Brent Scowcroft, *The Tower Commission Report: The Full Text of the President's Special Review Board,* 3; Jean Edward Smith, *The Constitution and American Foreign Policy;* and Louis Fisher, *Presidential War Power.*

three years of the Reagan presidency. The implementation of the new policy after 1984 is most properly the subject of another study.

While the book will not detail the momentous events of the late 1980s, it does contend that the 1984 policy reversal was the beginning of the ending of the cold war. As early as January 1984 Washington began to seek better relations with Moscow. This shift was the first small step on the road to ending the cold war. This is not to suggest, however, that the Reagan administration planned the demise of the cold war. At the time, such a revolution was virtually inconceivable. But the administration did seek to reduce hostilities and to open dialogue between the superpowers. It thus sought to place superpower relations on a more positive track.

The book also does not mean to suggest that Mikhail Gorbachev was not pivotal in bringing the cold war to its conclusion. Gorbachev was crucial, and it is unlikely that the cold war would have ended in the late 1980s without his reforms. However, while Gorbachev took the ball and ran with it, it was President Reagan who had put the ball in play.

Finally, this book has been written under a number of constraints. Most importantly, sensitive government documents from this period in U.S. history will not be released for twenty years. Therefore, the book is based upon documents that are currently accessible, as well as upon interviews with officials who were in office during the Reagan presidency. While the book's findings are necessarily tentative, evidence thus far suggests that its conclusions are compelling.

2

America's Soviet Policy, 1981–1985

> Let us . . . embark here and now upon renewed, open,
> and comprehensive East-West dialogue. Let us conduct
> ourselves in our deliberations so that historians of the
> future will mark this . . . as a turning point in East-West
> relations.
> —*Secretary of State George Shultz, January 17, 1984*[1]

CONVENTIONAL WISDOM HOLDS that the Reagan administration did not begin seeking better relations with Moscow until November 1985, when Ronald Reagan and Mikhail Gorbachev first met during the Geneva summit meeting. Reagan took a liking to Gorbachev, so this argument goes, and administration officials were impressed with the Soviet leader's reformist views. In response to Gorbachev's "new thinking," the Reagan administration became more conciliatory toward the Kremlin. According to this view, Washington changed its Soviet policy in response to changes taking place within the USSR.

This chapter seeks to demonstrate that the conventional view is inaccurate. The Reagan administration espoused a hard-line Soviet policy from 1981, when it came to office, through late 1983. In October 1983 Deputy Secretary of State Kenneth Dam delivered a speech on superpower relations that epitomized the administration's confrontational posture. This speech, however, marked the end of Reagan's hard-line period. Ten weeks later the administration reversed course.

---

1. George Shultz, Statement at the CDE in Stockholm, January 17, 1984, *DSB* (March 1984), 34–36.

On January 16, 1984, Washington began seeking a rapprochement with Moscow, calling for "cooperation and understanding" between the superpowers. These changes in U.S. policy could not have been a response to Gorbachev because they preceded him by more than a year.

This chapter will detail the changes in U.S. Soviet policy, focusing on the administration's image of the superpower relationship, its perception of the main threats to U.S. security, and its policy goals and strategies. As will be demonstrated, the Reagan administration not only changed its stated policy toward Moscow, but its assumptions about superpower relations as well.

U.S. Soviet Policy, 1981–1983

The Reagan administration based its Soviet policy on several assumptions about the Soviet Union and the nature of the superpower relationship (Table 1). Most fundamentally, the administration maintained that the Kremlin sought "world revolution and a one-world communist state." According to Reagan officials, communist ideology called for the global overthrow of democracy, and the conversion of all countries to a communist form of government. Since the leaders of the Soviet Union were communists, their aim was to promote such a global revolution. "They have told us that their goal is the Marxian philosophy of world revolution and a single one-world Communist state and they're dedicated to that," the president explained to Walter Cronkite in 1981. Two years later, Reagan reiterated these sentiments to convention-goers in Florida. "[A]s good Marxist-Leninists, the Soviet leaders have openly and publicly declared that the only morality they recognize is that which will further their cause, which is world revolution," he stated.[2]

2. Reagan, News Conference, January 29, 1981, *Public Papers of the Presidents: The Presidency of Ronald Reagan, 1981,* 57; Reagan, Interview with Walter Cronkite, March 3, 1981, *DSB* (April 1981), 9; Reagan, Remarks at the Annual Convention of the National Association of Evangelicals in Orlando, Florida, March 8, 1983, *Public Papers 1983,* 362. See also Alexander Haig, Breakfast Meeting with Newspeople, March 13,

Table 1
The Reagan Administration's Soviet Policy, 1981–1985

	1981–1983	1984–1985
Nature of Superpower Relations:	Zero-Sum Competition	Combination of Common Interests and Rivalry
Perceived Primary Threats:	Soviet Expansionism Soviet Military Strength	War Misunderstanding
Goals of U.S. Soviet Policy:	Soviet Restraint Soviet Reciprocity	Cooperation Understanding
Strategies:	Linkage Rebuild U.S. Military Strength Low Priority for Arms Control	Superpower Dialogue Emphasize Need for Global Arms Reduction Confidence-Building Measures

Because of the Soviet desire for global communism, the superpowers were locked in a zero-sum competition. The Kremlin sought to overthrow democratic governments throughout the world and to replace them with communist systems. Therefore, administration officials believed it was imperative for the United States to vanquish communism before communists vanquished the West. "The West won't contain communism, it will transcend communism," Reagan asserted during a 1981 commencement address. "It will dismiss [communism]

1981, *DSB* (May 1981), 11; and Reagan, News Conference, January 20, 1982, *Weekly Compilation of Presidential Documents [WCPD]* 18:64.

as some bizarre chapter in human history whose last pages are even now being written." During an address to the British Parliament the following year, the president predicted that "the march of freedom and democracy . . . will leave Marxism-Leninism on the ashheap of history. . . ."[3]

The competition between the superpowers was enduring, Reagan officials maintained. Competition was inherent in the superpowers' differing ideologies, and there was little likelihood that such rivalry could be resolved through diplomatic means. "The differences between the Soviet Union and the West are deeply rooted," Under Secretary of State for Political Affairs Lawrence Eagleburger explained in February 1983.

> The Soviets [are] not only our rival, but the rival of a humane world order. . . . Our rivalry, then, must continue as long as our two nations remain true to the principles upon which they were founded. . . . [N]o one man—indeed no group of men—can affect, except at the very margins, the fundamentally competitive nature of our relationship. . . . And I must caution you that improvements [in the superpower relationship], if they do come, are bound to be modest. We will not see the day of days with the Soviet Union. Our rivalry will, I fear, outlive all of us in this room.[4]

The Reagan administration also believed that the Soviet Union posed the main threat to American security. Moscow threatened the United States in two distinct, but related, ways. First, Washington charged that Soviet "expansionism" and "interventionism" threatened U.S. security. Reagan officials asserted that the Kremlin "promoted violent change" throughout the globe, especially in areas of "vital interest to the West." "Moscow is the greatest source of international insecurity today," Secretary of State Alexander Haig declared shortly after taking office. "Soviet promotion of violence as the instrument

3. Reagan, Commencement Address at Notre Dame, May 17, 1981, *WCPD* 17:532; Reagan, Speech to Members of the British Parliament, June 8, 1982, *DSB* (July 1982), 27.

4. Lawrence Eagleburger, "Review of U.S. Relations with the Soviet Union," February 1, 1983, *AFP:CD 1983,* 499–500, 504.

of change constitutes the greatest danger to world peace." Two years later Haig's successor, George Shultz, told the Senate Foreign Relations Committee that Soviet expansionism continued to be one of the greatest perils to global stability. Through its imperialistic behavior the Soviets had "needlessly drawn more and more international problems into the East-West rivalry," Shultz charged. Moscow's "unconstructive involvement, direct and indirect, in unstable areas of the Third World," and its "unrelenting efforts to impose an alien Soviet 'model' " on foreign countries threatened American security. "We have to make clear that we will resist encroachments on our vital interests and those of our allies and friends," Shultz urged the committee.[5]

The Reagan administration asserted that the Soviet Union's military strength also posed a threat. U.S. officials maintained that the Kremlin had been engaging in an "unremitting and comprehensive military buildup" since the 1960s. The Soviets had been devoting an increasing percentage of their gross national product (GNP) to military expenditures, the White House charged, using these resources to both expand and modernize its arsenal.[6]

The Soviet military buildup was threatening not only because of its sheer size, but also because of the intent behind it. The White House charged that Moscow had been building up for offensive purposes. "The Soviet Union has been engaged in the greatest military buildup in the history of man," Reagan asserted in August 1981, "and it cannot be described as necessary for their defense. It is plainly a buildup that is offensive in nature." Defense Secretary Caspar Weinberger agreed, cautioning that "it was neither reasonable nor prudent to view the Soviet military buildup as defensive in nature."[7]

5. Haig, "A Strategic Approach to American Foreign Policy," August 11, 1981, *DSB* (September 1981), 11; Haig, "A New Direction in U.S. Foreign Policy," April 24, 1981, *DSB* (June 1981), 6; Shultz, "U.S.-Soviet Relations in the Context of U.S. Foreign Policy," June 15, 1983, *AFP:CD 1983*, 509–10.

6. Reagan, Letter to Brezhnev, September 22, 1981, *DSB* (November 1981), 52; Reagan, Address to the National Press Club, November 18, 1981, *WCPD* 17:1275. See also Reagan, Address to the Nation, November 22, 1982, *WCPD* 18:1517–18; and Shultz, "U.S.-Soviet Relations," *AFP:CD 1983*, 509.

7. Reagan, Remarks at Rancho del Cielo, August 13, 1981, *WCPD* 17:874; "Excerpts from Weinberger Statement on Military Budget Outlay," *New York Times*, March 5, 1981.

Reagan officials dismissed the idea that the Kremlin might feel threatened by the United States, and had instituted a military buildup in response. "If there is any truth to the belief of some that the Soviet Union is motivated by fear of the West, that they think the West is going to threaten them . . . ," Reagan told journalists in 1982, "I don't think there's anyone in the West who believes that for one minute." The following year the president insisted that the "Soviet leaders know full well there is no political constituency in the United States or anywhere in the West for aggressive military action against them." Other officials echoed these sentiments. "[The Soviets] know perfectly well we'll never launch a first strike," Weinberger quipped in 1983. "I don't see how they can believe that." Secretary of State Shultz added, "such a perception [is] incredible, at least to us."[8]

Moreover, Reagan officials asserted that while the Soviets had been building up, the West had been building down. The result was a dangerous military imbalance. According to Reagan, the United States was militarily inferior to the USSR. "The truth of the matter is that on balance, the Soviet Union does have a definite margin of superiority," he declared in 1982, "enough so that there is risk and there is what I have called . . . 'a window of vulnerability.'"[9]

These fundamental assumptions about the Kremlin, the nature of the superpower relationship, and the main threats to U.S. security formed the foundation upon which U.S. Soviet policy was built. Such images not only shaped the Reagan administration's basic posture toward the Soviet Union, they largely determined the administration's policy goals and strategies. Washington formed its policy goals in

8. Reagan, Press Conference, May 21, 1982, *WCPD* 18:714; Keith L. Shimko, "Reagan on the Soviet Union and the Nature of International Conflict," 369; Shimko, *Images and Arms Control,* 80; George Shultz, *Turmoil and Triumph: My Years as Secretary of State,* 464.

9. Reagan, Press Conference, January 20, 1982, *WCPD* 18:61; Reagan, Press Conference, February 9, 1982, *WCPD* 18:182; Reagan, News Conference, March 31, 1982, *WCPD* 18:411; Reagan, Interview with the Media in Williamsburg, May 31, 1983, *DSB* (July 1983), 22. See also Reagan, Question and Answer Session with Reporters, April 5, 1982, *WCPD* 18:442; and Reagan, Question and Answer Session with Rockwell International Employees, May 25, 1982, *WCPD* 18:700, among others.

response to the perceived threats of Soviet expansionism and military strength. In order to check these dangers, Washington sought "Soviet restraint and Soviet reciprocity."[10] "Restraint" entailed an end to interventionism. The administration required "the Soviet Union [to] cease and desist from instigating, supporting, and carrying out efforts to effect historic change by force, whether it be done through proxy or the direct involvement of Soviet forces. . . ."[11] Under Secretary of State Eagleburger explained in 1983,

> The Soviet Union must observe certain basic standards of national conduct. . . . The Soviet occupation of Afghanistan, the suppression of the popular desire for reform in Poland, the Vietnamese imperial control of Kampuchea at the behest of the Soviet Union, their Cuban proxy's promotion of instability in Southern Africa and Central America, . . . all these acts demonstrate that the Soviets have . . . failed to abide by the rules of civilized societies. . . . [12]

Washington's aim was to arrest the expansion of Soviet communism.

"Reciprocity" was a more nebulous demand. At times it pertained to the making and fulfilling of international agreements. "What do we want of the Soviet Union?" Haig asked in the summer of 1981. "We want greater Soviet restraint on the use of force. We want greater Soviet respect for the independence of others. And we want the Soviets to abide by their reciprocal obligations, such as those undertaken in the Helsinki accords." At other times "reciprocity" implied cutbacks in the Soviet military arsenal. "We hope [the Soviets] move from

10. Among others, see the following, all by Haig, "A New Direction," *DSB* (June 1981), 6; News Conference in Manila, June 20, 1981, *DSB* (August 1981), 42; Interview for the *Wall Street Journal*, July 9, 1981, *DSB* (September 1981), 25; and "Overview of Recent Foreign Policy," November 12, 1981, *DSB* (January 1982), 16. See also Reagan, Letter to Brezhnev, *DSB* (November 1981), 52; William Clark, "President Reagan's Framework for Peace," October 29, 1982, *DSB* (December 1982), 33–34; and Eagleburger, "Review of U.S. Relations," *AFP:CD 1983*, 499–504.

11. Haig, News Conference in Manila, *DSB* (August 1981), 42. See also Haig, "A New Direction," *DSB* (June 1981), 6; and Clark, "Framework for Peace," *DSB* (December 1982), 33–34.

12. Eagleburger, "Review of U.S. Relations," *AFP:CD 1983*, 500–501.

an excessive reliance on expenditures for military purposes to those which are designed to . . . meet the needs of the Russian people and the non-Russian populations in the Soviet Union," Haig told journalists in 1981. "This would increasingly make the policies of the Soviet Union more compatible with the world view I talked about: restraint, reciprocity, acceptance of historic change by rule of law and not by force of arms."[13]

The Reagan administration implemented a three-pronged strategy for achieving Soviet restraint and reciprocity. First, it introduced a policy of "linkage." Washington maintained that any improvement in superpower relations was contingent upon a change in Soviet behavior. If Moscow did not demonstrate restraint and reciprocity, the United States would insure that there would be no improvements in East-West relations. "The most persistent troubles in U.S.-Soviet relations arise from Soviet intervention in regional conflicts, aggravating tensions, and hampering the search for peaceful solutions," Haig asserted in 1981. "Unless we can come to grips with this dimension of Soviet behavior, everything else in our bilateral relationship will be undermined. . . ."[14]

The Reagan administration initially linked three issues to Soviet international behavior. The first was East-West trade. "Over the past decade, [economic] ties [between the blocs] have grown rapidly," Haig explained, "but they have not restrained the Soviet use of force. The time has come to refashion East-West economic relations. . . . [W]e cannot have full and normal economic relations if [the Soviet leaders] are not prepared to respect international norms of behavior." Washington would restrict American exports and financial assistance to

13. Haig, "A Strategic Approach," *DSB* (September 1981), 12. For similar references, see others by Haig: "A New Direction," *DSB* (June 1981), 5–7; News Conference in Manila, *DSB* (August 1981), 42; Interview on "Face the Nation," June 28, 1981, *DSB* (August 1981), 51–52; Interview with *Wall Street Journal*, 25; "Overview of Recent Foreign Policy," November 12, 1981, *DSB* (January 1982), 16; and "Update on International Developments," March 2, 1982, *DSB* (April 1982), 33. See also Reagan, Letter to Brezhnev, *DSB* (November 1981), 52; Shultz, "U.S.-Soviet Relations," *AFP:CD 1983*, 509; Clark, "Framework for Peace," *DSB* (December 1982), 33–34; and Eagleburger, "Review of U.S. Relations," *AFP:CD 1983*, 499–504.

14. Haig, "A Strategic Approach," *DSB* (September 1981), 12.

the USSR if the Kremlin continued its "imperialist" activities abroad. National Security Adviser William Clark declared in late 1982, "For as long as the Soviet Union continues to . . . divert its resources into a massive military buildup, the United States—at a minimum—will not contribute to that process by providing the technology, hardware, or credits to make these Soviet tasks easier."[15]

Reagan officials also made summit meetings contingent upon Soviet behavior. In March 1981 Walter Cronkite asked the president whether he planned to hold a summit meeting with Soviet General Secretary Leonid Brezhnev. Reagan indicated that certain preconditions had to be met first. "I think that it would help bring about such a meeting if the Soviet Union revealed that it is willing to moderate its imperialism; its aggression [against] Afghanistan would be an example," he explained. "We could talk a lot better if there was some indication that they truly wanted to be a member of the peace-loving nations of the world, the free world. . . ." During a 1981 press conference Haig remarked, "[L]inkage is a prevailing concept in the administration, and . . . talks—the pace, the scope, and the level of them—will be determined by corresponding Soviet international behavior in the broadest sense of the term—that's the American policy."[16]

The White House placed a multitude of other stipulations on the talks, suggesting that it sought to avoid such meetings. For instance, the administration asserted that the president would only participate if the talks served a "real purpose" and entailed "legitimate negotiations." It also maintained that a summit meeting could not take place without extensive negotiating beforehand. Such a conference must be "carefully planned," the president contended. "And an agenda must be set, and that begins with a foreign ministers meeting." Reagan also repeatedly insisted that he could not accept a summit invitation without consulting American allies first. "The main thing is that you don't just call up and say: 'Yes, let's get together and have lunch,' " he reasoned. "A summit meeting of that kind takes a lot of preparation and the first preparation from our standpoint is the pledge that we've made to our

15. Ibid.; Clark, "Framework for Peace," *DSB* (December 1982), 33–34.

16. Reagan, Interview with Cronkite, *DSB* (April 1981), 9–10; Bernard Gwertzman, "U.S. Likely to Defer Meeting with Soviets on Control of Arms," *New York Times*, March 2, 1981.

allies that we won't take unilateral steps. We'll only do things after full consultation with them because they're involved also." (Reagan never indicated that he intended to engage in such consultations, however.) Haig maintained that there was so much preparatory work involved in a summit meeting that they "should only be used most sparingly." As a result of all these necessary preconditions, the administration rejected summit invitations from both Brezhnev and his successor, Yuri Andropov.[17]

The Reagan administration also initially tied arms control talks to Soviet international behavior. In April 1981 Haig asserted that it would serve "no useful purpose" to engage in arms talks with the Soviets while they continued their "imperialist activities abroad." Later that year the secretary explained, "We have learned that Soviet-American agreements, even in strategic arms control, will not survive Soviet threats to the overall military balance or Soviet encroachment upon our strategic interests in critical regions of the world. Linkage is not a theory; it is a fact of life."[18]

In the spring of 1982, however, the administration effectively de-coupled arms talks from Soviet international behavior. In May, the president announced that a new round of arms negotiations, the Strategic Arms Reduction Talks (START), would begin the following month. In making this announcement the president did not indi-cate that the Soviets had satisfied any of the preconditions that he had initially established. This led some to suggest that "linkage was dead." This was an overstatement, however. It is more precise to view Reagan's call for arms talks as a narrowing in linkage's scope. Although arms talks were no longer beholden to a change in Soviet behavior, East-West trade and summit meetings remained so.[19]

17. See Reagan, "Program for Economic Recovery and U.S.-Soviet Relations," February 24, 1981, *WCPD* 17:182–83; Reagan, News Conference, July 28, 1982, *WCPD* 18:966; Reagan, Interview with Cronkite, *DSB* (April 1981), 10; Haig, Inter-view with Ken Sparks, March 16, 1981, *DSB* (June 1981), 24; and David Hoffman, "President Pushed for Missile Defenses," *Washington Post,* November 22, 1985.

18. Haig, Interview with Sparks, *DSB* (June 1981), 24–25; Haig, "A Strategic Approach," *DSB* (September 1981), 12. See also Haig, "Relationship of Foreign and Defense Policies," July 30, 1981, *DSB* (September 1981), 18.

19. Reagan, Commencement Address at Eureka College, May 9, 1982, *WCPD* 18:603. For speculation on the end of linkage, see Bernard Gwertzman, "Major Shift

The second element in the Reagan administration's strategy for achieving Soviet restraint and reciprocity was an American military buildup. Believing that the USSR had military superiority, and that Moscow was building up for offensive purposes, the White House sought to revitalize U.S. military strength.

Reagan officials began the rebuilding process by increasing defense expenditures. In March 1981 the White House proposed the largest peacetime military budget in U.S. history. The administration advocated spending $222.8 billion on the American military in 1983, an increase of $33.8 billion. Reagan also proposed to increase defense spending by approximately 7 percent per year between 1981 and 1985, totaling over one trillion dollars. Defense expenditures would consume more than 30 percent of the federal budget over the next four years. The administration planned to use these resources to strengthen the American military posture in strategic forces, combat readiness, force mobility, and general-purpose forces.[20]

President Reagan also initiated the Strategic Defense Initiative (SDI) research program in March 1983. Believing that Moscow was building up for offensive reasons, the president sought to develop a defense against a Soviet nuclear attack. SDI would serve as a shield to protect Americans from incoming Soviet missiles. This shield would, in effect, mitigate the Soviet Union's military superiority over the United States.

The Reagan administration also decided to honor a 1979 NATO decision that called for the deployment of U.S. nuclear missiles in Europe. This "dual track decision," as the NATO agreement came to be known, had been made in response to the Soviet deployment of

---

by Reagan," *New York Times,* May 10, 1982; Reagan, Press Conference, May 21, 1982, *WCPD* 18:715–16; and Comments on Domestic and Foreign Policy Issues, May 24, 1982, *WCPD* 18:689–90.

20. Richard Halloran, "Reagan to Request $38B Increase in Military Outlays," *New York Times,* March 5, 1981; William M. Kaufmann, *A Reasonable Defense,* 25. See also Reagan, Remarks at Dinner for the Conservative Political Action Conference, February 26, 1982, *WCPD* 18:237; and Budget Message to Congress, February 8, 1982, *WCPD* 18:139. These expenditures were especially striking given that the administration's foremost priority was to reduce the federal budget. Reagan was slashing spending in all other sectors.

mobile SS-20 missiles that were aimed at Western Europe. It called for the NATO allies to pursue arms limitation talks with the Warsaw Pact in order to reduce the SS-20 threat. At the same time, however, the United States would deploy intermediate-range Pershing II and cruise missiles in Western Europe to counterbalance the Soviet SS-20s. The deployment of these missiles was scheduled to begin in late 1983.

The Reagan administration's third strategy for achieving Soviet restraint and reciprocity was to give arms control issues low priority. "Arms control is no longer the centerpiece of U.S.-Soviet relations," Haig asserted in the summer of 1981. "The centerpiece must be what contributes to the security of the American people, to international peace and stability. . . ." Because it believed the Soviets were militarily superior, the Reagan administration was reluctant to enter into arms talks. Such talks might also have threatened the administration's military buildup. In March 1981 the president postponed "for a month or two" a Standing Consultative Commission meeting that would have been the first U.S.-Soviet meeting on arms control since he took office. Since there had only been one postponement of a SCC meeting since 1972, and then only for two days, this move was highly symbolic and set the tone for early arms control relations.[21]

Reagan also initially rejected the unratified Strategic Arms Limitation Treaty (SALT II) as "fatally flawed." Rather than encouraging Soviet restraint and reciprocity, he argued, the agreement bolstered the military imbalance. Reagan charged that SALT II "allowed the Soviet Union to just about double their present nuclear capacity." Moreover, verification was dubious. Because of allied and domestic pressure, however, the administration did ultimately decide to abide by the terms of the treaty.[22]

Dissatisfied with the SALT process, and under pressure to show a commitment to arms control, Reagan proposed a new arms reduction

21. Haig, Appearance on ABC's "Issues and Answers," July 19, 1981, *DSB* (September 1981), 24; Gwertzman, "U.S. Likely to Defer Meeting," *New York Times*, March 2, 1981.

22. Reagan, News Conference, January 29, 1981, *DSB* (March 1981), 12. See also Steven R. Weisman, "Reagan Willing to Broaden Talks on Nuclear Arms," *New York Times*, May 14, 1982. The administration discontinued this practice on December 31, 1985, the date on which SALT II would have lapsed had it been ratified.

plan in November 1981, the so-called "zero option." This proposal called for the elimination of all intermediate-range nuclear forces in Europe. Since the Soviets were the only ones who had such weapons in Europe at the time, Reagan's proposal was rather inequitable. (While NATO did have plans to deploy intermediate-range missiles in Europe, deployment was not scheduled to begin for two years.) Administration officials privately acknowledged that they knew Moscow would reject the zero option since it required much more of the Kremlin than it did of the West. As expected, the Soviets rejected the offer, calling it a "propaganda ploy."[23]

President Reagan also proposed a new series of arms negotiations, the Strategic Arms Reduction Talks (START). Although he proposed the START talks in November 1981, the president declined to begin the negotiations until June 1982. Reagan unveiled the U.S. negotiating position for the START talks during a spring speech in Eureka, Illinois. Once again, the proposals were hardly equitable. The president proposed that land- and sea-based warheads should be reduced to the same number on each side, and of that amount no more than 2,500 missiles could be land-based. Since the Soviets had about 5,500 land-based warheads and the United States only 2,152, this plan required Moscow to destroy over half its arsenal while Washington could continue to build up. Moreover, Moscow relied primarily on its land-based missiles for its deterrent. Reducing them by half would have assuredly weakened its position vis-à-vis the West.[24]

The zero option and the Eureka proposal were distinctly one-sided plans. Washington made little effort to address Soviet concerns, or to offer proposals that Moscow could find remotely acceptable. This strongly suggested that the Reagan administration was not genuinely interested in arms control. As a result, rather than facilitating negotiations, these proposals stymied the arms control process.

23. Reagan, "Arms Reduction and Nuclear Weapons," November 18, 1981, *WCPD* 17:1273; Leslie Gelb, "Reagan to Propose Missile Terms," *New York Times*, November 17, 1981; "Reagan's Arms Proposal Assailed," *Current Digest of the Soviet Press [CDSP]* 33:47, 7.

24. Reagan, Eureka College, May 9, 1982, *WCPD* 18:603; Gwertzman, "Major Shift by Reagan," *New York Times,* May 10, 1982.

In sum, U.S. policy toward the Soviet Union was highly confrontational between 1981 and 1983. The Reagan administration believed that Moscow sought the global conversion to communism. Consequently, the superpowers were locked into a zero-sum competition for spheres of influence. Washington also perceived Moscow to be the primary threat to American security, and therefore demanded significant changes in Soviet behavior. It offered little in return, however. Rather than enticing the Soviets to change their policies with promises of improved relations, Washington sought to penalize the Kremlin. Relations would not improve until Moscow conformed.

Deputy Secretary Dam's Speech on U.S.-Soviet Relations

On October 31, 1983, Deputy Secretary of State Kenneth Dam delivered a speech on U.S.-Soviet relations that epitomized the administration's early hard-line policy. The occasion for the address was the fiftieth anniversary of the establishment of diplomatic relations between the United States and the Soviet Union.[25]

Dam's speech came in the midst of a tension-filled autumn. On September 1 a Soviet military plane had shot down Korean Airlines Flight 007 killing all 269 people aboard, including 61 Americans. When the Kremlin denied all knowledge and responsibility for the tragedy, President Reagan had become enraged, calling the incident a "crime against humanity." A previously scheduled meeting between Secretary Shultz and Soviet Foreign Minister Andrei Gromyko that month went on as planned, but was especially acrimonious. On September 28 General Secretary Andropov issued an unusually bitter statement saying, in effect, that Moscow had given up trying to improve relations with the Reagan administration.

Dam's speech typified the administration's early assumptions about the Kremlin and superpower relations. In it he asserted that Moscow sought worldwide revolution and charged that the Kremlin engaged in "adventurism and intimidation" as a means for promoting the expansion of communism. He spoke at length about the threat such

25. Dam, "Challenges of U.S.-Soviet Relations," *DSB* (December 1983), 26–30.

interventionism posed to U.S. security. Washington, he said, had "heightened concerns" about the Soviets' "increasingly disruptive international behavior over the past decade." He then catalogued some perceived Soviet transgressions.

> In recent years we have seen . . . the Soviet Union's direct military intervention into Afghanistan; its strengthened economic and military involvement with such regional powers as Cuba and Vietnam and its active support for the occupation of Kampuchea; deployment of over 20,000 . . . military personnel in more than 30 Third World countries, . . . [and] its extensive use of sur-rogate forces—some 40,000 Cuban military personnel are in Angola, Ethiopia, and Central America, not to mention Grenada.

Dam also asserted that the USSR was "the largest arms exporter to the Third World and the principal supplier of over 34 states, twice as many as a decade ago."

As was custom for Reagan officials, the deputy secretary devoted a significant portion of his speech to the Soviet military buildup. He charged that the Kremlin had been devoting increasingly larger percentages of its GNP to the development of weaponry. "The Soviet military sector has first claim on raw materials, transportation re-sources, personnel, and capital equipment," he insisted. "More than one third of all Soviet machinery output now goes to the military and about one half of all research and development expenditures are for military applications." Like other administration officials before him, Dam asserted that the Soviet buildup was not motivated by defensive concerns. "The scope and persistence of the Soviet Union's efforts to create an instrument of military power beyond plausible defense requirements are troubling," he remarked. The Kremlin was building an offensive "military machine," Dam charged, not a defensive arsenal.

Dam also spent considerable time detailing the perceived imbalance in military arsenals.

> Over the past decade . . . the Soviets have manufactured approxi-mately 2,000 new intercontinental ballistic missiles [ICBMs]; by comparison, the United States built approximately 350 during the same time. The Soviets built 54,000 new tanks and armored

vehicles; U.S. production was 11,000. The Soviet Union turned
out 6,000 tactical combat aircraft; the United States, 3,000. The
Soviets launched 61 attack submarines; the United States, 27.

The Soviets had also "dramatically" improved the quality of their
weapons, he asserted.

The deputy secretary was emphatic that the Soviets' interventionism and military buildup were not merely in response to perceived
threats from the United States. "Occasionally we hear the argument
that Soviet patterns of behavior . . . are at least in part a response to
recent U.S. policies," Dam acknowledged. "It is asserted that Soviet
actions . . . have arisen out of deep-seated fears exacerbated by a
perceived U.S. hostility. While this circular action-reaction model of
U.S.-Soviet relations has a simplicity and a symmetry that may appeal
to those so inclined, the evidence available does not support it. . . .
Soviet activism in various Third World areas appears to be far more
opportunistic than defensive in the face of any supposed American
provocation."

In response to the twin threats of Soviet expansionism and the
Soviet military buildup, Dam called for Soviet restraint and reciprocity.
The West should "strive to create an environment in which the
Soviet Union is faced with . . . drastically reduced opportunities and
incentives for adventurism and intimidation," he argued. "In such
an environment we expect that over time the Soviets will see greater
restraint on their part as the most attractive option. . . ."

Furthermore, the deputy secretary declared that an improvement
in superpower relations would be dependent upon a change in Soviet
international behavior—something he did not expect to happen soon.
Moscow would have to abandon its military buildup, its expansionism, and its "quest for absolute security" before there could be any
warming in the relationship. Such progress, Dam suggested, was
not on the immediate horizon. While he acknowledged that there
had been a number of "modest developments" in the superpower
relationship during the summer of 1983, such as the signing of
a long-term grain agreement, Dam played down their significance.
"Contrary to some press speculation," he remarked, "[these modest
steps] did not constitute a sudden warming in the relationship, nor

were they a prelude to an early summit meeting. . . . The Soviets have not yet responded in any way to reduce tensions." Consequently, a superpower rapprochement was not in sight. "We are now in a period of uncertainty as to the immediate future of U.S.-Soviet relations," he observed. "We should be wary of illusions about the possibility of quick or dramatic breakthroughs."

U.S. Soviet Policy, 1984–1985
President Reagan's Address, January 16, 1984

Only ten weeks after Dam warned against any sudden warming in the superpower relationship, the Reagan administration reversed course and began seeking a rapprochement with Moscow. On January 16, 1984, President Reagan delivered an address on U.S.-Soviet relations that introduced striking changes to U.S. policy. Written primarily by Soviet experts rather than the more conservative White House speechwriters who usually penned Reagan's speeches, the address signaled a change in the administration's assumptions about the Kremlin, the superpower relationship, and the primary threats to U.S. security.[26] It also introduced new policy goals and strategies.

In his address Reagan revealed significant changes in the administration's understanding of the Kremlin and superpower relations. Strikingly, the president played down the ideological rivalry between the superpowers. In earlier years the administration had focused on the ideological differences between the two countries, and the zero-sum competition that had ensued from these differences. In January 1984 Reagan abruptly changed course. He now focused on what the two countries had in common. The president spoke repeatedly of the superpowers' "common interests," and asserted that such interests

26. Soviet expert Jack Matlock was instrumental in writing the president's January 16 address while Shultz, McFarlane, and Reagan also drafted sections of the speech (McFarlane, interview with author, July 7, 1995; Weinberger, phone interview with author, July 31, 1995; and Matlock, phone interview with author, September 19, 1995).

should supersede ideological disagreements. "Neither we nor the Soviet Union can wish away the differences between our two societies and our two philosophies," he intoned. "But we should always remember that we do have common interests. . . ." Foremost among these common interests was the desire for peace. But there were other shared concerns as well, Reagan suggested, such as poverty, disease, and the desire to provide for each nation's children. The president drove home this point in the conclusion to his speech, which he wrote himself.

> Just suppose with me for a moment that an Ivan and Anya could find themselves, say, in a waiting room or sharing a shelter from the rain or a storm with a Jim and Sally, and there was no language barrier to keep them from getting acquainted. Would they then deliberate the differences between their respective governments? Or would they find themselves comparing notes about their children and what each other did for a living? Before they parted company they would probably have touched on ambitions and hobbies and what they wanted for their children and the problems of making ends meet. And as they went their separate ways, maybe Anya would say to Ivan, "wasn't she nice, she also teaches music." Maybe Jim would be telling Sally what Ivan did or didn't like about his boss. They might even have decided that they were all going to get together for dinner some evening soon.

Soviet and American leaders should focus on their common humanity, Reagan declared, not their ideological rivalry.

In his address Reagan also emphasized that the United States posed no threat to Soviet security. "Our challenge is peaceful," he declared. "We do not threaten the Soviet Union. . . . Our countries have never fought each other; there is no reason why we ever should." This statement reflects two fundamental changes in the Reagan administration's conception of the superpower relationship. First, prior to this address, Reagan officials had dismissed the idea that Moscow could feel threatened by the United States. Only ten weeks earlier Deputy Secretary Dam had stated explicitly that such an idea was nonsensical. Reagan's remarks suggest that he had come to accept that the Kremlin could view Washington as a potential aggressor. Second, before this speech the president had spoken of the U.S.-Soviet relationship in Manichaean terms. The "freedom-loving and democratic" West was morally obligated to engage in the struggle against the "evil empire."[27] There was a moral imperative to fight against communism because democracy's very existence was at stake. The president's new assertion that there was "no reason" why the two countries should ever fight stands in stark contrast to these earlier sentiments.

The administration's assumptions about the Kremlin and the superpower relationship formed the foundation upon which U.S. Soviet policy was built. Since these assumptions changed in early 1984, so, too, did the administration's understanding of the primary threats to American security. In his January 16 address the president no longer asserted that Soviet expansionism and military strength were the main threats to U.S. security. Rather, he emphasized the threat of war. He discussed this threat in general terms, without pinning it to any one country. "Reducing the risk of war—and especially nuclear war—is priority number one," he declared. "A nuclear conflict could well be mankind's last." Because of the "vast stockpiles of arms in the world" there was an increased likelihood that political disagreements would evolve into armed conflict. This endangered global security, Reagan suggested.

The president also spoke of "dangerous misunderstandings and miscalculations" that threatened American security. Reagan was rather ambiguous regarding the exact nature of these "misunderstandings," but he suggested they were related to the threat of war. The "gap in Soviet and American perceptions" of international affairs was "so great," he asserted, that the likelihood of conflict was increased. The United States needed to reduce not only nuclear arsenals, but the chances for misunderstanding as well, he argued. More specifically, the countries had to find "meaningful ways to reduce the uncertainty and potential for misinterpretation surrounding military activities, and to diminish the risk of surprise attack."

President Reagan also introduced new policy goals during his January 16 address. The president no longer saw Soviet expansionism and military strength as the main threats to U.S. security. Therefore,

27. Reagan, Remarks to Evangelicals, *Public Papers 1983*, 55.

the United States no longer sought Soviet restraint and reciprocity. The main threats to the United States were now the threat of war, and what Reagan called "dangerous misunderstandings." Consequently, the president sought "cooperation and understanding" with the Soviet Union. "We must establish a better working relationship," Reagan declared, "one marked by greater cooperation and understanding." The superpowers should "rise to the challenges facing us and seize opportunities for peace," he asserted.

Reagan's call for cooperation and understanding was a significant change in U.S. Soviet policy. For one thing, it reversed the administration's earlier confrontational posture toward the Kremlin. The focus was no longer on condemning Soviet international behavior and demanding that the Kremlin conform to American standards. Rather, Washington now focused on the need to peacefully resolve international problems. The president's call for cooperation in solving global conflicts also implied that Washington had accepted the Soviet Union as a superpower and an equal. This was a significant shift from the administration's earlier posture that, by demanding changes in Soviet international behavior, had implied that the USSR was subordinate to the United States.

In his January 16 address Reagan introduced a strategy for attaining cooperation and understanding between the superpowers. The first element of this strategy was the institutionalization of superpower dialogue. "We must and will engage the Soviets in a dialogue as constructive as possible," declared the only president in forty years never to have met his Soviet counterpart. "[H]igh level consultations [should] become a regular and normal component of U.S.-Soviet relations." The aim of these meetings would be to reduce the threat of war and to rectify misunderstandings. "We seek genuine cooperation, [and] cooperation begins with communication," Reagan announced, "In our approach to negotiations, reducing the risk of war—and especially nuclear war—is priority number one." Notably, the president did not link these talks to changes in Soviet international behavior. This directly contradicted the administration's earlier position on summit meetings.

Reagan's call for dialogue held a sense of urgency, as was evident in his assertion that Washington "must and will" enter into talks with the Kremlin. The president also proclaimed, "The fact that neither of us likes the other's system is no reason not to talk. Living in the nuclear age makes it imperative that we do talk." This is an interesting justification for the need for dialogue. Ronald Reagan had been living in the nuclear age since taking office, indeed, since President Truman had been in office. Yet, despite this, he had avoided a summit meeting for the first three years of his presidency. In fact, he had rejected summit invitations from both Soviet General Secretary Brezhnev, and his successor, Yuri Andropov.[28] This suggests that it was not simply "the nuclear age" that inspired Reagan to so eagerly seek a summit conference.

The second part of Reagan's new strategy was an increased emphasis on arms reduction. The president devoted a significant portion of his address to the need "to stop arms races around the world." "Nuclear arsenals are far too high," he insisted. The superpowers needed to join together and "accelerate" efforts to conclude arms reduction agreements. Reviewing his earlier proposal to eliminate intermediate-range nuclear missiles, Reagan added, "Indeed, I support a zero option for all nuclear arms . . . [M]y dream is to see the day when nuclear weapons will be banished from the face of the Earth."

It is noteworthy that Reagan devoted only one paragraph of his speech to Soviet violations of existing arms agreements. In the past, this had been a sore issue with the administration, and numerous officials had denounced the Kremlin for "stretching treaties to the brink of violation and beyond."[29] In this address the president tread softly around the issue. "Cooperation and understanding are built on deeds, not words," he said. "Complying with agreements helps; violating them hurts. . . ." Strikingly, the president suggested that Soviet transgressions might not have been entirely willful, and indicated that some of the problems may have stemmed from "ambiguities" in the accords. The fault was not with the Kremlin, Reagan implied, it was in the treaties themselves.

28. David Hoffman, "President Pushed for Missile Defenses," *Washington Post*, November 22, 1985.
29. Shultz, "U.S.-Soviet Relations," *AFP:CD 1983*, 509; Dam, "Challenges of U.S.-Soviet Relations," *DSB* (December 1983), 28.

Confidence-building measures were the third part of the strategy for attaining cooperation and understanding. In his address Reagan began calling for measures that could "reduce the threat and use of force . . . in regional conflicts." Rather than denouncing the Kremlin's "expansionist" activities, Reagan stated that the superpowers "should jointly examine concrete actions that we can both take to reduce U.S.-Soviet confrontation" throughout the world. "A durable peace requires ways for both of us to defuse tensions and regional conflicts," he argued. "Would it not be better and safer if we could work together to assist people in areas of conflict in finding peaceful solutions to their problems? That should be our mutual goal."

The manner in which President Reagan redirected U.S. Soviet policy can be seen most vividly in Table 2. This chart compares the percentage of lines the president devoted to specific topics in U.S.-Soviet relations during his address, to the percentage of lines Deputy Secretary Dam devoted to the same topics ten weeks earlier. The differences are striking.[30]

Dam devoted 61 percent of his speech to Soviet expansionism and the Soviet military buildup. The president allocated a mere 5 percent of his address to these issues. Moreover, Reagan did not once use the terms "expansionist," "interventionist," or "adventurist," despite the fact that these were recurring phrases in earlier statements by administration officials.

Dam had also been skeptical about arms control. He implied that the United States needed to build up its military in order to match Soviet strength, and charged the Kremlin with contravening existing arms control treaties. The deputy secretary saw no pressing need to

30. This content analysis used the deputy secretary's speech and the president's address as published in the *DSB*. Therefore, the typeface and spacing is the same for both. Each line of the respective speeches was coded according to whether the speaker was referring to one of the following: the Soviet military buildup, Soviet expansionism, the need for arms reduction, the need for cooperation, the need for dialogue, common interests between the superpowers, and misunderstandings and/or the need for better understanding between the two countries. Some lines may have referred to more than one topic, and therefore, may have been coded twice. Other lines were not coded at all because they dealt with subjects not under examination.

Table 2
Comparative Content Analysis of Dam Speech and Reagan Speech
(Percentage of lines referring to key issues in U.S.-U.S.S.R. relations)

Reference	Dam Speech Oct. 31, 1983	Reagan Speech Jan. 16, 1984
Soviet Military Buildup	37	2
Soviet Expansionism	24	3
Need for Arms Reduction	0	16
Common Interests	0	19
Need for Cooperation	0	17
Need for Dialogue	1	13
Misunderstanding/ Need for Understanding	0	7

pursue new arms agreements. President Reagan, on the other hand, believed there was an urgent need to move the arms control process forward. Consequently, he devoted 16 percent of his address to the need for arms reduction.

There is another striking difference. In January 1984 Reagan devoted a full 19 percent of his address to the superpowers' common interests. Ten weeks earlier, Dam had made no such allusions. Instead, Dam argued that it would continue to be difficult to build a constructive relationship "with a nuclear superpower whose interests and values are so different from our own." Moreover, Dam did not once call for cooperation between the superpowers, whereas Reagan devoted 17 percent of his address to such issues.

There are also some qualitative differences between the two speeches that should be noted. Dam's scant references to "dialogue" revolved mainly around detailing the administration's past contacts with Soviet officials. He did not indicate that there was a pressing *need* for dialogue. Nor did he suggest that the administration was actively pursuing dialogue with the Soviet Union. Rather, Dam simply suggested that Washington would be "open" to the idea if Moscow were to pursue it. The tone of President Reagan's many references to the need for dialogue was entirely different. The president asserted that there was an "imperative" need for East-West communication and implied this was a matter of utmost urgency.

The Reagan administration went to great lengths to signal that the president's January 16 address was an important one. White House officials held several press briefings about the speech the week before it was given, and touted the speech as a significant change in direction. In a highly unusual move, aides released excerpts of the address to the press days in advance.[31]

Despite such efforts, Reagan's address was not widely recognized as an important shift in policy. One reason for this is that the president's speech came at the outset of a presidential election year. Many of the major American newspapers dismissed the speech as election-year rhetoric. Moscow agreed. Calling the speech "devoid of new ideas or constructive proposals," the Kremlin suggested that it was aimed at the ballot box. "These words are clearly a sop to short-term calculations," Soviet Foreign Minister Gromyko grumbled to the press.[32]

Another reason the policy change went unrecognized is that superpower relations remained rocky in the months immediately following Reagan's address. Both capitals were facing pressing domestic concerns, and could therefore devote little time to foreign affairs. The Kremlin was experiencing a rapid turnover in leadership. General Secretary Yuri Andropov passed away in February 1984, and his successor, Konstantin Chernenko, became seriously ill himself soon

31. Michael Getler, "Positive Tone May be Change of Tune," *Washington Post,* January 17, 1984.

32. For example, see David Ignatius, "White House Set for Election-Year Effort at Improving U.S.-Soviet Relationship," *Wall Street Journal,* January 16, 1984; Hedrick Smith, "Reagan's Address: Trying a New Tactic," *New York Times,* January 17, 1984; and Lou Cannon, "U.S. Nuclear Arms Have Made World Safer, Reagan Says," *Washington Post,* January 17, 1984. "Reagan Speech on Soviet Ties Called Propaganda," *CDSP* 36:3, 4; "Gromyko Assails U.S. Foreign Policy," *CDSP* 36:3, 3.

after taking office. For its part, the Reagan administration's most pressing priority was the upcoming presidential election. Although the administration continued to seek cooperation and understanding, concrete actions toward this end were somewhat limited until the presidential campaign was over.

It is clear, however, that President Reagan's January 16 address was not simply an aberration. Rather, it was a turning point in the administration's approach to Moscow. Reagan introduced lasting changes to U.S. Soviet policy. When one examines U.S. policy through the 1985 Geneva summit meeting, the conference that is usually recognized as the official beginning of the end of the cold war, it is clear that the Geneva summit was simply the culmination of the policies Reagan had introduced in early 1984.

Washington Continues to Seek Cooperation and Understanding

Throughout 1984 and 1985 the Reagan administration continued to focus on the superpowers' shared interests rather than their ideological differences. For instance, the president used his 1984 address to the United Nations to underscore the superpowers' common interests. Looking toward the Soviet delegation, Reagan reminded the audience of the "great common ground upon which we all stand: our fellowship as members of the human race, our oneness as inhabitants of this planet, our place as representatives of billions of our countrymen whose fondest hope remains the end to war and to the repression of the human spirit. These are the important central realities that bind us, that permit us to dream of a future without the antagonisms of the past." Reagan then went on to argue that politics often creates artificial barriers to understanding. Political divisions only obscure the ties that bind people together. "I leave you with a reflection from Mahatma Gandhi," he said in conclusion, "spoken with those in mind who said that the disputes of the modern world are too great to overcome."

> I am not conscious of a single experience throughout my three months' stay in England and in Europe that made me feel that after all East is East and West is West. On the contrary, I have

been convinced more than ever that human nature is much the same, no matter under what clime it flourishes, and that if you approached people with trust and affection, you would have ten-fold trust and thousand-fold affection returned to you.[33]

"We're all God's children," Reagan asserted the following year, "with much in common."[34]

Administration officials also continued to emphasize that the United States posed no threat to the USSR. In March 1984 President Reagan wrote his first letter to the new Soviet general secretary, Konstantin Chernenko, and used the opportunity to underscore Washington's peaceful intentions. "I understand some people in the Soviet Union feel a genuine fear of our country," he began, "but I cannot understand why our programs would seem threatening. . . . Perhaps our policies have been misunderstood in Moscow. . . . The United States has no desire to threaten the security of the Soviet Union." In an address to the Irish Parliament several months later, Reagan again asserted Washington's benign intentions. "We remain ready for [the Soviets] to join with us and the rest of the world community to build a more peaceful world," he declared. "In solidarity with our allies, confident of our strength, we threaten no nation." During an academic meeting in the autumn of 1984, Secretary Shultz reiterated, "We must persuade the Soviets . . . that we have no aggressive intentions. We mean no threat to the security of the Soviet Union."[35]

After January 1984 the Reagan administration spoke infrequently of the Soviet military buildup or expansionism. War, and especially nuclear war, was the main threat to American security. "A nuclear war

33. Reagan, Address to the United Nations, September 24, 1984, *AFP:CD 1984*, 220, 227.

34. Reagan, "Hopes for the Geneva Summit," November 14, 1985, *AFP:CD 1985*, 425.

35. Reagan, *An American Life*, 595–96; Reagan, Address to the Irish Parliament, June 4, 1984, *DSB* (August 1984), 18; Shultz, "Managing the U.S.-Soviet Relationship over the Long Term," October 18, 1984, *AFP:CD 1984*, 454. See also Shultz, Statement on the President's Meeting with Soviet Foreign Minister Gromyko, September 28, 1984, *AFP:CD 1984*, 448; and Bernard Gwertzman, "Gromyko Meetings End with Accord on Further Talks," *New York Times*, September 30, 1984.

cannot be won and must never be fought," the president repeatedly proclaimed. Officials continually asserted that "the vast numbers of nuclear armaments in the world" rendered nuclear war more likely. In November 1984 Reagan commented,

> I just happen to believe that we cannot go into another generation of the world living under the threat of those weapons and knowing that some madman can push the button some place. It doesn't have to be one of the superpowers. A war could be triggered, as nuclear weapons proliferate, by someone else doing it.[36]

The administration also continued to emphasize the dangers of misunderstandings in international relations. Shortly after the president's January 16 address, Secretary Shultz devoted an entire speech to the need to "reduce the danger of surprise attack, miscalculation, or misunderstanding" between nations. Shultz declared that Washington sought "measures to increase openness and improve communication [in order] to provide . . . greater insurance against miscalculation." During an address to the United Nations later in the year the president drove home the same message. There was an urgent need to correct "miscalculations" in the superpower relationship, he argued, because they increased the "potential risk of U.S.-Soviet confrontation."[37]

Washington continued to seek a rapprochement with Moscow. During a 1984 speech in Stockholm, Shultz repeated the president's call for a "better working relationship between the United States and the Soviet Union, one marked by greater cooperation and understanding." Reagan reiterated this theme during a February 1984 radio address.

36. See Reagan, Address to the UN, *AFP:CD 1984,* 220–27; Shultz, Statement at the CDE, *DSB* (March 1984), 34–36; and "An Interview with the President," *Time,* November 19, 1984, 36.

37. Shultz, Statement at the CDE, *DSB* (March 1984), 34. Reagan, Address to the UN, *AFP:CD 1984,* 225. This speech was dramatically different from the hardline speech Reagan had delivered to the UN in 1983. For more detail, see Steven R. Weisman, "Reagan at UN, Asks Soviet for Long-Term Framework to Press for Arms Control," *New York Times,* September 25, 1984.

"I emphasize once again America's desire for genuine cooperation between our two countries," he remarked. "Together we can help make the world a better, more peaceful place."[38]

In an effort to attain cooperation and understanding, the Reagan administration fervently pursued dialogue with the Kremlin throughout 1984 and 1985. "We believe in dialogue and in solving problems," Shultz declared in 1984. "We believe in realistic and meaningful engagement with others to advance the cause of peace. . . . Let us . . . embark here and now upon renewed, open, and comprehensive East-West dialogue. Let us conduct ourselves in our deliberations that historians of the future will mark this . . . as a turning point in East-West relations." At the February 1984 funeral of Soviet leader Yuri Andropov, Vice President George Bush repeated, "Living together in this nuclear age makes it imperative that we talk to each other, discuss our differences, and seek solutions to the problems that divide us." Bush also "conveyed the president's determination to move forward in all areas of our relationship with the Soviets, and our readiness for concrete, productive discussions."[39]

During a news conference in June 1984 the president repeated his strong desire to have a summit conference with General Secretary Konstantin Chernenko. "We're ready, willing, and able" to meet with the Soviet leadership, Reagan declared. "I am willing to meet and talk anytime." More importantly, the president softened the preconditions in order for such a meeting to take place. Originally he had tied a conference to Soviet international behavior, and had asserted that the United States would have to consult with its allies before it would consent to a summit meeting. The administration had also asserted that such a meeting would have to have a specific agenda. These conditions no longer applied. Moreover, whereas the goal of a summit meeting had been to produce concrete results, the aim now was simply to gain a better understanding of each other. Reagan remarked,

38. Shultz, Statement at the CDE, *DSB* (March 1984), 35; Reagan, Radio Address to the Nation, February 11, 1984, *AFP:CD 1984*, 413.
39. Shultz, Statement at the CDE, *DSB* (March 1984), 35–36; "Bush: 'We Too Want Deeds,'" *Washington Post*, February 15, 1984.

I'm not talking about a preconstructed meeting in which you've got a list of points. You can have an agenda in which it is the general idea of things that you think could lead to better understanding. And that's good enough for me. . . . Now, if they agree with me that there are things we can talk about that might clear the air and create a better understanding between us, that's fine.[40]

In September 1984 the president repeated his call for the institutionalization of cabinet-level meetings between the two countries. These discussions would focus "on the whole agenda of issues before us, including the problem of needless obstacles to understanding," Reagan stated. "I believe such talks could work rapidly toward developing a new climate of policy understanding, one that is essential if crises are to be avoided and real arms control is to be negotiated." "We can't accomplish anything talking about each other," the president declared later that month. "We have to talk to each other."[41]

The Reagan administration also continued to stress the need for arms reduction throughout 1984 and 1985. In January 1984 Shultz reiterated "the American commitment to reduce the vast stockpiles of arms in the world," and introduced a new proposal for the "complete and verifiable elimination of chemical weapons on a global basis."[42] In his September 1984 address to the United Nations, Reagan introduced a new framework for arms negotiations that was the antithesis of his earlier policy of linkage. "[W]e need to extend the arms control process to build a bigger umbrella under which it can operate—a road map if you will, showing where, during the next 20 years or so, these individual efforts can lead," he explained. "If progress is temporarily halted at one set of talks, this newly established framework for arms control could help us take up the slack at other negotiations."[43]

Moreover, the Reagan administration took a more collaborative approach to arms control than it had in earlier years. Before 1984

40. Reagan, News Conference, June 14, 1984, WCPD 20:830, 852–53.

41. Reagan, Address to the UN, AFP:CD 1984, 226; Lou Cannon and David Hoffman, "Soviet's Visit Set in Secrecy," Washington Post, September 30, 1984.

42. Shultz, Statement at the CDE, DSB (March 1984), 36. See also Reagan, Address to the UN, in ADP:CD 1984, 224.

43. Reagan, Address to the UN, AFP:CD 1984, 226.

the White House had been in the habit of putting forth one-sided proposals which would have allowed the United States to build up its military while requiring the Soviets to dismantle parts of their arsenal. This was no longer to be the case. "Our approach," Reagan stated, "will be designed to take into account concerns the Soviet Union has voiced."[44]

The White House also indicated a willingness to reduce the levels of U.S. armaments. For example, in his September 1984 meeting with Gromyko, Reagan offered "strategic trade-offs" to the Soviets if they would resume the START talks. This implied that Washington was willing to reduce its arsenal of heavy bombers and air-launched cruise missiles, where there was a U.S. advantage, in return for a Soviet reduction in land-based ICBMs, where they had the advantage. Washington's proposals were no longer intended solely for American gain.[45]

It cannot be argued that the Reagan administration brought about a breakthrough in arms negotiations by the end of 1985. Although arms talks resumed in March 1985, little progress had been made by the end of the year.[46] But what is important for the present purposes is the administration's stated position regarding arms control. By 1985 the Reagan administration was pursuing arms control more actively than it ever had, and more realistically. Rather than offering one-sided proposals, it had begun to negotiate.

The White House also continued to call for confidence-building measures so as to reduce the likelihood of superpower conflict. In July 1984 Washington and Moscow agreed to modernize the hot line used for crisis communications. A facsimile system would be added so that the capitals could communicate much more rapidly during crises. Such communications would take one-third of the time they had previously taken. Reagan hoped that the improved hot line would address both the problems of war and misunderstanding. "[This is] a modest but positive step toward enhancing international stability," he

44. Ibid.
45. Cannon and Hoffman, "Soviet's Visit," *Washington Post*, September 30, 1984.
46. In December 1983 the Soviets had broken off all arms control talks in response to the arrival of the U.S. Pershing II and cruise missiles in Europe.

remarked during the signing ceremony, "and [toward] reducing the risk that accident, miscalculation, or misinterpretation could lead to a conflict" between the superpowers.[47]

Later that year Reagan called for a series of talks between the superpowers so as to discuss confidence-building measures. "Spheres of influence are a thing of the past," the president declared. "Together we have a particular responsibility to contribute to political solutions to [regional conflicts]. . . . History displays tragic evidence that it is these conflicts which can set off the sparks leading to worldwide conflagration." The president recommended periodic consultations among senior experts in order to discuss regional disputes. "The objectives of this political dialogue will be to help avoid miscalculation, reduce the risk of U.S.-Soviet confrontation, and help the people in areas of conflict to find peaceful solutions," he asserted.[48]

The Geneva Summit Meeting, November 1985

Although the Geneva summit meeting is often seen as the beginning of the end of the cold war, it was actually the culmination of the new Soviet policy that Reagan had introduced in January 1984. The Geneva summit embodied the administration's commitment to dialogue, cooperation, and understanding. Moreover, it took place only eight months after Gorbachev had become leader of the Soviet Union. He had not yet introduced *glasnost* and *perestroika,* and no one could foresee at that time how revolutionary the new Soviet leader would prove to be. The American approach to the Geneva summit meeting, therefore, could not have been merely a response to changes in Soviet policies.

As already noted, the Reagan administration had been very evasive about a summit conference prior to 1984. In 1985, however, it was President Reagan who initiated the Geneva summit. On March 10, 1985, the Kremlin announced that Konstantin Chernenko had passed

47. Robert S. Greenberger, "Reagan Approves Accord Upgrading Hot Line for Crises," *Wall Street Journal,* July 18, 1984.
48. Reagan, Address to the UN, *AFP:CD 1984,* 222, 225.

away. Within hours of learning that Gorbachev would be the new Soviet leader, the Reagan administration invited him to a summit meeting. No preconditions were attached. There was no agreed-upon agenda. There was no certainty that any concrete agreement would result from the conference. In fact, the administration did not yet know what Gorbachev's policy positions would be. The Reagan administration had extended an invitation to a summit meeting solely because the administration felt there was an imperative need for dialogue.

The White House hoped the Geneva summit would address the threats to American security. The meeting would help reduce the threat of war and help to clarify "dangerous misunderstandings." "My mission, stated simply, is a mission for peace," the president remarked as he departed for Geneva. "It is to engage the new Soviet leader in what I hope will be a dialogue for peace that endures beyond my presidency." Through dialogue the leaders of the two countries would facilitate understanding and cooperation. Reagan explained,

> It is my fervent hope that the two of us can begin a process which our successors and our peoples can continue—facing our differences frankly and openly and beginning to narrow and resolve them; communicating effectively so that our actions and intentions are not misunderstood; and eliminating the barriers between us and cooperating wherever possible for the greater good of all.[49]

"Formal agreements are not the important thing," Shultz remarked. "The important thing is that we understand each other." Another aide added, "The president believes this can be a watershed meeting [if both sides] hear each other out and begin to understand each other better."[50]

The administration also hoped to convince Soviet leaders that the United States posed no threat to the security of the Soviet Union.

49. Reagan, "Hopes for the Geneva Summit," *AFP:CD 1985*, 423.
50. David B. Ottaway and Celestine Bohlen, "Shultz Terms Soviet Talks 'Good First Step,'" *Washington Post*, August 1, 1985; Lou Cannon and David Hoffman, "Possible Accord on Arms Talks Seen," *Washington Post*, November 19, 1985.

Explaining why he had invited Gorbachev to a meeting, Reagan remarked to journalists, "They themselves, just like us, they've got suspicions that they think are legitimate with regard to our intent." Years later, the president elaborated on what he had hoped to achieve at Geneva. "During [my first] five years [in office] I had come to realize there were people in the Kremlin who had a genuine fear of the United States. I wanted to convince Gorbachev that we wanted peace and they had nothing to fear from us."[51]

During the summit meeting Reagan underscored his commitment to dialogue. Despite the fact that only a fifteen-minute meeting between the two leaders had been scheduled beforehand, the president wound up consulting one-on-one with the Soviet leader for nearly five hours. Reagan spent more time talking with Gorbachev than he had with any other world leader. The most notable achievement of the Geneva meeting was an agreement to institutionalize dialogue. The leaders agreed to hold two more summits over the next two years.

Despite the administration's new emphasis on the need for arms reduction, the summit did not yield any new arms agreements. Reagan proposed a 50 percent reduction in strategic offensive arms and the eventual elimination of intermediate-range missiles in Europe, which Gorbachev found acceptable. However, the Soviet leader would not consent to any of these proposals until Washington agreed to abandon the Strategic Defense Initiative. Reagan refused, arguing that SDI would be for defensive purposes only. He also offered to share SDI research with the Soviets, but Gorbachev found these arguments unconvincing. As a result, there were no historic breakthroughs in arms control.

Although the Geneva summit produced little in the way of specific accords, both sides portrayed the meeting to be a great success. Reagan officials described it as "very worthwhile" and noted the "friendly mood and good atmosphere." The Soviets called the meeting

51. Rowland Evans and Robert Novak, "Reagan's Softening Soviet Line," *Washington Post*, April 3, 1985. Reagan, *An American Life*, 12. Reagan made similar comments as he was leaving for the Geneva summit meeting. See Reagan, Remarks before Departing for Geneva, November 14, 1985, *AFP:CD 1985*, 426.

a "watershed." "Because of the Geneva summit," Gorbachev declared, "the world has become a more secure place."[52]

Conclusions

On January 16, 1984, the Reagan administration abruptly abandoned its hard-line policy toward the Soviet Union and began calling for a rapprochement between the superpowers. The administration's assumptions about the Kremlin, superpower relations, and the primary threats to U.S. security changed dramatically. So, too, did the administration's goals and strategies. In many respects, these changes represented a wholesale reversal from the administration's initial confrontational posture toward Moscow. Washington's new conciliatory policy led directly to the Geneva summit meeting in November 1985. Although the Geneva summit is commonly viewed as the beginning of the end of the cold war, it is clear that the meeting had its roots in the policies that Reagan had introduced in early 1984.

This argument contradicts prevailing views regarding the U.S. role in bringing about the end of the cold war. Conventional wisdom holds that the Reagan administration became more conciliatory only in response to changes within the Soviet Union. Such an idea is mistaken. President Reagan delivered his turning-point address fifteen months before Mikhail Gorbachev became leader of the USSR. Washington reversed course *before* Moscow began to reform.

It is not clear why the Reagan administration reversed its Soviet policy. The only rationale the White House offered was that "living in the nuclear age" made dialogue "imperative." This reasoning is unconvincing. Reagan officials had refused summit meeting invitations

---

52. The superpowers signed agreements on cultural exchanges and air safety in the Pacific and agreed to open new consulates in Kiev and New York. However, the two countries had been near agreement on these commitments for over a year. See Dam, "Challenges of U.S.-Soviet Relations," *DSB* (December 1983), 29. See also Lou Cannon, "Gorbachev Sincere, Reagan Tells Aides," *Washington Post,* November 23, 1985; Hoffman and Oberdorfer, "Gorbachev Agrees to Visit," *Washington Post,* November 21, 1985; and Celestine Bohlen, "Gorbachev Discusses 'Lively' Exchanges," *Washington Post,* November 22, 1985.

for the first three years they were in office—despite the fact that they were living in the nuclear age. Therefore, other factors must have precipitated the abrupt change in policy.

It is also not clear why the Reagan administration changed U.S. policy in the manner it did. Some of the themes that the president introduced in 1984 are not easily explicable. For example, the repeated references to "dangerous misunderstandings" are curious. Reagan officials never clarified what misunderstandings they were referring to, and it is unclear what the White House would hope to gain by introducing such a theme. It is also not obvious why the administration began to so urgently pursue superpower dialogue. The White House had avoided summit meetings for three years. Why, beginning in 1984, was it "imperative" to hold such talks? The administration's frequent statements that the United States "posed no threat" to the Soviet Union are also not easily explicable. For what purpose would the administration introduce such a theme? This policy change is especially puzzling because it is much more common to assume that others understand one means them no harm. It is unusual to recognize that others may question and fear one's intentions. The administration's earlier position, in which it dismissed the notion that the Kremlin might feel threatened by the United States, was more the norm. "It takes great insight to realize that actions that one believes to be only the natural consequence of defending one's vital interests can appear to others as directed against them," Robert Jervis has noted.[53] What caused the Reagan administration to have such insight? This is the central question of the following chapters.

---

53. Jervis, *Perception and Misperception*, 354.

Public Opinion and Foreign Policy Making
The Impact of the 1984 Presidential Election

I**N JANUARY 1984, THE REAGAN ADMINISTRATION** abruptly changed its Soviet policy; the White House abandoned its confrontational posture and began seeking a rapprochement with Moscow. Washington no longer sought Soviet "restraint and reciprocity." Rather, its new goal was "cooperation and understanding" between the superpowers. What caused the Reagan administration to reverse its Soviet policy in 1984? Any hypothesis must be assessed in terms of three criteria. First, it should state exactly what caused the administration to reevaluate its standing policy and to switch course. Second, the explanation must explain the timing of the policy change, spelling out why the Reagan administration reversed course in the ten weeks between Deputy Secretary Dam's speech of October 31, 1983, and President Reagan's address of January 16, 1984. Finally, the hypothesis must explain why U.S. policy changed in the manner it did. It should spell out why the Reagan administration chose to reverse course, rather than to simply modify its existing policy; why officials began speaking of "dangerous misunderstandings" and the "imperative" need for dialogue; and why officials began insisting that the U.S. "posed no threat" to the security of the Soviet Union.

Many political observers have maintained that the Reagan administration altered its Soviet policy in 1984 in order to strengthen the president's prospects for reelection. "President Reagan has been nagged by his campaign handlers to wash out his mouth when he talks about the Soviets," *Washington Post* columnist Mary McGrory commented three days after Reagan's turning point address. "They forced him into making a speech, which they said in advance was going to be 'conciliatory.' All he said before he was dragged kicking and screaming into the East room was that he wouldn't call the Soviet Union an 'evil empire' anymore. . . . He was performing a campaign chore, which he apparently hoped his conservative core constituency would forgive and forget."[1]

While many shared McGrory's belief that Reagan's January 16 address was election-year propaganda, few expressed their views as explicitly. Many simply assumed that the Reagan administration altered its Soviet policy in order to appeal to more voters, and proceeded to analyze Reagan's address in light of such assumptions. Lou Cannon's seminal book on the Reagan presidency is an example. In *President Reagan: The Role of a Lifetime,* Cannon discusses the president's 1984 address on U.S.-Soviet relations. He even suggests that it was a distinct change in tone. But Cannon does not discuss this pronouncement in his rather lengthy section on the administration's Soviet policy. Rather, he deals with it in his chapter on Reagan's reelection campaign. The assumption, of course, is that the speech was campaign rhetoric and nothing more.[2]

McGrory and Cannon are in esteemed company. Joseph Nye of Harvard has drawn the same conclusions about Reagan's address. "With the onset of an election, the president was drawn back to the center," Nye has argued. "By moving from confrontation to the middle of the road, and by stressing the prospect of cooperation [with the Soviet Union], the president cut off an important avenue of attack for his Democratic opponent. In short, the Reagan administration policy toward the Soviet Union began to change for American domestic political reasons. . . ."[3]

1. Mary McGrory, "Despite His Handlers' Hype, Reagan Didn't Sound Converted," *Washington Post,* January 19, 1984.

2. Lou Cannon, *President Reagan: The Role of a Lifetime,* 507–10; "Campaign '84: Warming up for the Kickoff," *Newsweek,* January 30, 1984, 14–15.

3. Joseph S. Nye, "Gorbachev's Russia and U.S. Options," 392. For similar views, see Michael Mandelbaum and Strobe Talbott, *Reagan and Gorbachev,* especially 40; Seyom Brown, *The Faces of Power: United States Foreign Policy from Truman to Clinton,* 483–502; and Raymond Garthoff, *Great Transition: American-Soviet Relations and the End of the Cold War,* 142.

There were a number of factors that caused observers to conclude that the administration's about-face was motivated by electoral concerns. One was the timing of the policy shift. Reagan reversed his approach to Moscow in January 1984, less than ten months before the presidential election. Not only was the speech delivered at the outset of an election year, it came just as the primary season was about to begin. The first caucus in Iowa was to be held in four weeks, and the New Hampshire primary was scheduled for February 28, 1984.[4]

Moreover, Reagan's address coincided with a highly publicized debate among the Democratic contenders for the presidency. On January 15, 1984, the Democrats staged their largest debate up to that time. Held in New Hampshire, where the first primaries would soon take place, all eight Democratic contenders participated. News anchorman Ted Koppel and talk-show host Phil Donahue moderated the nationally televised debate and, as analysts predicted, it attracted a large audience. The main topic of discussion, moreover, was arms control and superpower relations. Since the Democrats were expected to criticize the Reagan administration's management of superpower relations, critics argued that the president's speech was simply an effort to draw attention away from the Democrats' forum.[5]

Observers concluded that the election was behind the policy shift for another reason: many believed that Reagan's foreign policy was his Achilles' heel. While the president's domestic policies were popular, some argued that his approach to international affairs was a source of concern for many Americans. The president's foreign policy record was dragging down his overall approval ratings, they argued.[6]

4. Michael Getler, "Positive Tone May Be Change of Tune," *Washington Post,* January 17, 1984.

5. The contest for the Democratic candidate for president had been under way for months. By January 1984 there were already eight contenders, some of whom had been campaigning since April 1983. They were: former Florida governor Reubin Askew, Senator Alan Cranston, Senator John Glenn, Senator Gary Hart, Senator Ernest F. Hollings, the Reverend Jesse Jackson, former presidential candidate and Senator George McGovern, and former vice president Walter F. Mondale.

6. See James Reston, "Straws in the Whirlwind," *New York Times,* December 11, 1983; Hedrick Smith, "Reagan's Address: Trying a New Tactic," *New York Times,*

The number of Americans who approved of Reagan's overall job performance throughout his first term was never high by historical standards. The president's approval ratings for his first two years in office were significantly lower than Jimmy Carter's ratings for the first half of his presidency. Moreover, Richard Nixon had garnered more public support during his first three years in the White House than Reagan was ever able to attain during his first term.[7]

Initially, Reagan's lack of public support was attributed to the sluggish American economy. As the recession of 1981–1982 set in, the president's approval ratings declined precipitously. White House officials were not overly concerned at the time, however, believing that the president's popularity would rise as the economy began to recover. Economic indicators suggested that a recovery would commence in the first half of 1983, in plenty of time for the election.[8]

To a certain extent, economic recovery did bolster the president's approval ratings. In July 1983 a number of polls registered a rise in Reagan's popularity. Most attributed this to an increase in the number of people who commented favorably on his handling of the economy. Reagan's campaign strategists were gratified with the results, feeling their original predictions had been validated. "Those voters who went a little soft during the hard times are coming back," the president's pollster, Richard Wirthlin, commented in July 1983.[9]

January 17, 1984; Cannon, *President Reagan,* 508–9; and Don Oberdorfer, *The Turn: From Cold War to New Era,* 70.

7. "The President and the Polls," *Washington Post,* May 20, 1983. Reagan had a 58 percent approval rating his first year in office. In both his second and third years in office, 44 percent of those polled approved of the way he was handling his job. In comparison, Jimmy Carter had a 62 percent approval rating his first year, 46 percent in his second year, and 38 percent in his third year. In his first year as president Richard Nixon garnered a 61 percent approval rating. In his second year in office this fell to 57 percent, and in his third year 50 percent approved of the way he was handling his job. See *The Gallup Poll: Public Opinion, 1984,* 23.

8. The president's average approval rating for the year dropped fourteen percentage points between 1981 and 1982 (ibid.).

9. For example, a CBS/*New York Times* poll found a 22 percent increase between January and July 1983 in the number of people who felt President Reagan's programs had helped the economy. A July poll for Garth Analysis registered a ten-point jump in one month in Reagan's overall approval ratings. See Hedrick Smith, "Public's Approval

However, by late summer some polls indicated that Reagan's popularity had begun to plateau. The improving economy was not giving the president the boost his advisers had expected. Americans had turned their attention elsewhere. Reassured about the economy, they were instead worrying about foreign relations, some polls indicated. The August 1983 *Washington Post*/ABC poll found that 49 percent of those polled disapproved of the way Reagan handled foreign affairs, and 42 percent approved. This was the president's worst rating on foreign policy in seventeen surveys. "With the economy boosting his appeal but foreign policy working against him," the *Post* remarked, "Reagan seems to be at a political standstill." The *New York Times* echoed these sentiments. Its polls indicated that the president's overall approval rating was "rising, but limited." The small increase was attributed to "rising public confidence in the president's economic program." But this survey also suggested that Reagan was most vulnerable on foreign policy issues. "There was considerable evidence of unease about his foreign policies," reported Hedrick Smith. "A majority felt the president 'had not done enough' to reach an agreement with Moscow to reduce nuclear weapons." Smith's colleague, James Reston, concurred. Reagan was "beginning to scare the American . . . people with his dukes-up attitude toward the Russians and his adventures in Lebanon," he observed.[10]

Some argued that in order to bolster his chances for reelection the president had to mollify these concerns. Reagan had to adopt a more conciliatory posture toward the Soviets. Political scientist Robert W. Tucker argued that the American people wanted a two-track Soviet policy. "If our experience in recent years conveys one clear lesson," Tucker asserted, "it is that the public will not support a policy that does not hold out the hope of improvement in our relationship with the Soviet Union, and that does not actively seek improvement." The president had to be firm in his relations with the Kremlin, but he also

of Reagan in Poll Rising but Limited," *New York Times,* July 3, 1983; and "Washington Wire," *Wall Street Journal,* July 29, 1983.

10. Barry Sussman, "Perceptions: Poll Gives President Contrasting Remarks," *Washington Post,* August 8, 1983; Smith, "Public's Approval," *New York Times,* July 3, 1983; Reston, "Straws," *New York Times,* December 11, 1983.

had to be willing to make concessions in order to promote peace. Pollster Daniel Yankelovich agreed, adding, "Reagan has proved that he can be tough, but he has not yet proved that he can be a peacemaker. It is unlikely that this issue will escape bitter and partisan debate in an election year."[11]

There was a third factor that caused observers to dismiss the policy shift as election-year rhetoric. In early 1983 Reagan trailed the Democratic contenders for the presidency in many of the polls attempting to forecast the election outcome. Opinion polls indicated that voters preferred both John Glenn and Walter Mondale to Reagan. The White House feared the Democrats would seize upon Americans' growing apprehension about foreign policy, some argued, and thus increase their lead in the polls. During the 1980 presidential election Ronald Reagan had struck a chord with voters when he asked them, "Are you any better off now than you were four years ago?" Reagan officials feared that the Democrats might fare just as well in 1984 by asking, "Are you any safer now than you were four years ago?" "If the Democrats have any chance to win," one Republican strategist commented in 1984, "they have to reinforce the doubts about Reagan as a world leader, as a peacekeeper."[12]

By the end of 1983 the Democrats had begun to tailor their campaigns to address public concerns regarding Reagan's conduct of foreign affairs. They focused on Americans' growing unease over the prospect of war. When asked about the number one problem facing the United States, Walter Mondale spoke of the "nuclear menace" and the "survival of humanity." "If those bombs were to go off," he commented, "nothing else would matter." Likewise, John Glenn asserted that the foremost problem confronting the United States was the Reagan administration's "drift toward war."[13]

As did many Americans, the Democratic candidates charged that the president had not done enough to stop the nuclear arms race. They

11. Robert W. Tucker, "Toward a New Détente," 93; Otto Friedrich, "The View from the Street Corner," *Time*, January 2, 1984, 31.

12. Hedrick Smith, "One Campaign Issue Dominates: The Leadership of Ronald Reagan," *New York Times*, January 30, 1984.

13. Bernard Weinraub, "An Interview with Former Vice President Walter F. Mondale," *New York Times*, December 26, 1983; David Shribman, "An Interview with John Glenn, Senator and Former Astronaut," *New York Times*, December 27, 1983.

emphasized the fact that the Soviets had walked out of the Geneva arms talks in response to the Reagan administration's deployment of missiles in Europe. They then proposed ending this stalemate through various arms reduction plans of their own.

The Democratic candidates also focused on the president's conduct of superpower relations. Walter Mondale made much of the fact that Reagan was the only president never to have met with his Soviet counterpart. "There hasn't been a serious discussion with the Soviet Union, with heads of state . . . really since 1974," he remarked. "And that's very, very dangerous." In order to make relations more stable, Mondale advocated the institutionalization of annual summit meetings between the United States and the Soviet Union. This stood in sharp contrast to Reagan's longstanding avoidance of such meetings. Jesse Jackson also emphasized the need for expanded contacts between the Soviet Union and the United States. "We need an American president who will be glad to meet the head of the Soviet Union anywhere, any time, unconditionally," he asserted.[14]

Thus, some argue, the Reagan administration found itself in a bind. In early 1983 a number of polls suggested that the president was trailing his Democratic opponents. And the Democrats were beginning to focus their campaigns on Reagan's perceived weak spot—his conduct of foreign policy. The smartest thing to do, so this argument goes, was for the president to change his foreign policy and take the wind out of the Democrats' sails. "Mr. Reagan appears to be in a no-lose position in terms of domestic politics," David Ignatius remarked in the *Wall Street Journal* just after the president's turning-point address. "By extending the olive branch toward Moscow as the election year begins, he is likely to blunt charges by political opponents that he has allowed U.S.-Soviet relations to deteriorate to their lowest level in decades. If the Soviets spurn his initiative, it will probably strengthen the appeal of Mr. Reagan's usually hard-line rhetoric."[15]

14. Weinraub, "Interview with Mondale"; Ronald Smothers, "An Interview with the Reverend Jesse Jackson," *New York Times,* December 28, 1983.

15. David Ignatius, "White House Set for Election-Year Effort at Improving U.S.-Soviet Relationship," *Wall Street Journal,* January 16, 1984. See also James Reston, "Reagan's Political Strategy," *New York Times,* January 18, 1984; and Rowland Evans

On the surface, it seems plausible that changes in the United States' Soviet policy were implemented in an attempt to strengthen President Reagan's chances for reelection. However, closer inspection reveals that this argument is not fully explanatory. First of all, it does not adequately explain the catalyst for the policy change. This explanation assumes that public opinion caused the Reagan administration to reverse its Soviet policy. The relationship between public opinion and foreign policy decision making has been the subject of much debate, however. It is not at all clear whether public opinion leads policy makers, or whether policy makers lead public opinion. The early literature on public opinion and foreign policy asserted that Americans' attitudes had little impact on the making of foreign policy. Analysts such as Walter Lippmann and Gabriel Almond argued that Americans knew and cared little about foreign affairs. Such matters were too remote from their everyday lives. Consequently, presidents had a relatively free hand when making foreign policy. The executive could develop policy on the basis of officials' views and privileged information. It was then the president's role to lead the country in the direction he thought best. According to this view, the public is "an entity to be educated rather than a lodestar by which to be guided."[16]

Vietnam War–era scholars began to challenge this top-down view of foreign policy making. Many asserted that earlier studies had been flawed, and argued that public opinion on foreign policy was more stable, more rational, and less susceptible to elite manipulation than had been previously suggested. Analysts began advocating a "bottom-up" model of public opinion and foreign policy. In this view, "the public has a measurable and distinct impact on the foreign policy making process. In sum, leaders follow the masses."[17]

---

and Robert Novak, "The Week Reagan Played His Trump," *Washington Post,* January 18, 1984.

16. Ole R. Holsti, "Public Opinion," 444. See also Page and Shapiro, *Rational Public;* Risse-Kappen, "Public Opinion"; Nincic, "United States"; and Daniel Yankelovich and Richard Smoke, "America's 'New Thinking.'"

17. Risse-Kappen, "Public Opinion," 480. See also Benjamin I. Page and Robert Y. Shapiro, "Effects of Public Opinion on Policy"; Page and Shapiro, "Foreign Policy and the Rational Public"; and Cortright, *Peace Works.*

The bottom-up view has also been criticized, however. At times, foreign policy decisions are made without a clear consensus among the public. In such cases public opinion cannot determine policy outcomes. More importantly, there is still very little empirical evidence about the causal link between public opinion and foreign policy. Although many studies have examined the *correlation* between public attitudes and policy, few have demonstrated that public opinion has actually *caused* an administration to select a particular policy option. Consequently, the debate over the relationship between public opinion and foreign policy continues.

It is likely that presidents differ in their approach to public opinion. Some may prefer to make policy on the basis of public attitudes, in the belief that such methods are more democratic. Others may prefer to base foreign policy on the advice of government experts, and then to persuade the public that such policies are most effectual. Ronald Reagan clearly fell into the second camp. Reagan was not a poll-driven leader. Although the president was an amiable man, he was also rather stubborn when it came to questions of principle or ideology. Consequently, he had a distinct tendency to gamble with public opinion. Reagan "took many positions," biographer Lou Cannon writes, "most notably in supporting the contras and in opposing abortion, where [White House] polls found him out of step with American public opinion." Other scholars agree with Cannon's assessment. In his study of the Reagan administration's decision to intervene in Lebanon, Philip Powlick found that public opinion was a more salient issue for midlevel officials than it was for those higher up. Powlick concluded that Defense Secretary Weinberger was the only high-level official who carefully considered public attitudes when making policy recommendations. For Ronald Reagan, Secretary of State George Shultz, and National Security Adviser Robert McFarlane, public opinion was rather inconsequential when it came to formulating U.S. policy.[18]

Reagan's aides concur. The president "did not accept that extensive political opposition doomed an attractive idea," Shultz has observed. "He would fight resolutely for an idea, believing that, if it was valid,

18. Cannon, *President Reagan*, 445; Powlick discussed in Holsti, "Public Opinion," 454–55.

he could persuade the American people to support it. . . . He would do what he felt was right for the country, whether it was popular or not." On this issue, Caspar Weinberger agrees with Shultz. "The president believed that it was his role to inform public opinion," the defense secretary has confided. "He maintained that he should lead public opinion in the direction he wanted to go, and he was superb at doing that."[19] National Security Adviser Richard Allen agrees. "Ronald Reagan, as I have known him, has never been a man who was led by public opinion polls, but always sought to lead public opinion," commented Reagan's longtime friend.

> Richard Wirthlin, who is the president's pollster but has known him for a long time, would be the first to tell you that Ronald Reagan sees accurate poll taking and the pulse of public opinion as a tool to lead rather than an indication that he ought to change policies. . . . For instance, the fact that the majority of the people opposed aid to the contras only reinforced him in his belief, and you can find countless examples of this in Ronald Reagan.[20]

Reagan also consistently opposed the idea of a nuclear freeze, despite the fact that approximately 80 percent of Americans endorsed a freeze on the building, testing, and deployment of nuclear weapons.[21]

Throughout early 1983 some advisers were indeed encouraging the president to be more accommodating toward the Kremlin on the grounds that such a change would bolster his chances for re-election. Chief of Staff James Baker and Assistant to the President Michael Deaver, both pragmatists, were concerned that voters were growing skittish over the president's tough rhetoric. Nancy Reagan was especially concerned about her husband's prospects for reelection and repeatedly appealed to her husband to be more forthcoming to Moscow. Reagan adamantly rejected such arguments, however. The president had been a devoted hard-liner since his Hollywood days

19. Shultz, *Turmoil and Triumph,* 1135. Weinberger interview, July 31, 1995.
20. Robert L. Pfaltzgraf and Jacquelyn K. Davis, *National Security Decisions: The Participants Speak,* 84.
21. Page and Shapiro, *Rational Public,* 272.

in the 1940s, and he stubbornly maintained that it was his role to convince the public that his approach was in America's best interests. "The president would have willingly lost the second election if it came down to changing his Soviet policy," McFarlane has confided. Reagan would not compromise his principles in exchange for a second term in office.[22]

In short, for better or worse, President Reagan did not base his foreign policy on public attitudes. Adamant in his views, and convinced of his speech-making capabilities, the president sought to convert Americans to his own views. It would have been highly uncharacteristic for Reagan to have abandoned the hard-line posture that he had espoused for decades in order to cater to public opinion. And in fact, those close to him say he was prepared to lose the election rather than to change his policy.

There is another flaw in the argument that Reagan was simply responding to public opinion. The findings from polls taken during 1983 were highly ambiguous, and frequently contradictory. One would have been hard pressed to draw concrete policy conclusions from them. For one thing, it was not at all clear that Reagan was on the political defensive during 1983. For example, while some polls indicated that the president's popularity was leveling off during the summer, others did not. The Gallup Organization found Reagan's overall approval rating to be steadily increasing throughout 1983, except for a 2 percent decline between September and October. In fact, between October and December, there was a sharp 9 percent jump in Reagan's approval ratings.[23]

Reagan's position vis-à-vis the Democratic presidential candidates was also subject to interpretation. As noted, Reagan trailed the Democrats in the polls throughout much of 1983. However, many analysts failed to note that this gap was steadily closing throughout the second half of the year. In May a Gallup poll found the president to be trailing Senator Glenn by seventeen points. By September this had fallen to six points, and by December, Reagan was four percentage points ahead of

22. McFarlane interview, July 7, 1995. See also Shultz, *Turmoil and Triumph,* 317.
23. Gallup 1984, 23.

Glenn.[24] Polls showed the race between Reagan and Walter Mondale to be close, but the leader depended upon which poll one consulted. Some surveys had Reagan starting to edge out Mondale in August 1983, while others found the race to be flip-flopping throughout the autumn.[25]

This steadily closing gap between Reagan and the Democratic presidential candidates is noteworthy because it occurred before Reagan had announced his intention to seek a second term. The president began gaining on the Democratic contenders in the summer of 1983—long before he had begun to campaign for reelection. The Democrats, on the other hand, had been actively campaigning for months. This suggests that Reagan was a rather strong candidate, not the floundering incumbent that some portrayed him to be. Even more significant is the fact that Reagan was closing in on his opponents *without a change in his Soviet policy.* If the president's position vis-à-vis the Democrats was improving without a shift in his approach to Moscow, it is unclear why he would decide to switch to a more conciliatory Soviet policy.

Public attitudes about the Reagan administration's foreign policy were especially ambiguous, and could therefore have been interpreted in a number of ways. As many pointed out, Americans were more supportive of the president's domestic policies than they were of his conduct of foreign affairs. This led to the assertion that foreign policy was Reagan's Achilles' heel. However, some polls indicated that

24. The Gallup Organization found the following: May 1983: Glenn over Reagan: 54 percent to 37 percent; September 1983: Glenn over Reagan: 48 percent to 42 percent; December 1983: Reagan over Glenn: 49 percent to 45 percent. See "Glenn Leads Mondale," *New York Times,* May 19, 1983; *Gallup 1983,* 210; and *Gallup 1984,* 56.

25. Both the *Washington Post*/ABC poll and the Harris Survey found Reagan to be in a dead heat with Mondale in August 1983. See Sussman, "Perceptions," *Washington Post,* August 8, 1983; and Bill Peterson, "Pollster Sees Sign of Sweep by Dems," *Washington Post,* September 12, 1983. The Gallup poll found Reagan ahead of Mondale by three points in September (47 percent to 44 percent). In October Mondale had the lead (50 percent to 44 percent). By December Reagan had regained a seven-point lead (51 percent to 44 percent). See *Gallup 1983,* 208; and *Gallup 1984,* 54, 56.

support for the administration's foreign policy was actually growing throughout 1983. For example, in August Gallup found that 31 percent of its respondents approved of the president's handling of foreign policy. By October this had risen to 44 percent, and by November 46 percent approved. This was Reagan's highest approval rating on foreign policy in two years.[26] If it was true that Americans were growing more supportive of the administration's handling of foreign relations, there would seem little reason to change it.

Even more noteworthy is the fact that the approval rating for Reagan's Soviet policy was rising throughout 1983. In August Gallup found 41 percent of respondents approved of the way in which the president conducted relations with Moscow. In October this figure rose three percentage points, and by November 46 percent approved of his handling of relations with the USSR. Gallup also found in November that significantly more respondents approved of the president's handling of nuclear disarmament negotiations than disapproved (47 percent compared to 37 percent). These increasingly favorable ratings on Reagan's Soviet policy cast serious doubt on the assertion that the administration shifted its approach simply in order to win votes. The administration was gaining additional support without changing its policy.[27]

Other surveys also found a majority of Americans supporting the president's approach to the Soviet Union. In January 1984 a *Washington Post* survey concluded that "much of the public accepts the Reagan view that the Soviet Union or other hostile nations are mostly responsible for the tension that has become alarming to so many Americans." In early 1984 the Public Agenda Foundation found that 56 percent of its respondents agreed that "the Soviet Union is like Hitler's Germany—an evil empire trying to take over the world." The same percentage believed that "wherever there is trouble in the world—in the Middle East, Central America or anywhere else—chances are the Soviets are behind it." In addition, a *Time* magazine poll discovered that 82 percent of respondents agreed with the assertion that "the Soviets are constantly testing us, probing for weaknesses

26. Gallup 1984, 64–65.
27. Ibid.; and *Gallup 1983*, 262.

and they're quick to take advantage whenever they find any." Seventy-three percent agreed that "the Soviets treat our friendly gestures as weaknesses," and a majority asserted that "every sign of Soviet influence must be contained by military force if necessary."[28]

It is also worth noting that while approval ratings for Reagan's hard-line conduct of Soviet policy were steadily increasing, support for his policies in Lebanon and Central America was declining precipitously. In the autumn of 1983 Gallup conducted a survey on Americans' attitudes toward different aspects of the Reagan administration's foreign policy. It inquired about policies toward Grenada, the Soviet Union, Central America, and Lebanon, among others. The only issue areas in which a majority of the respondents disapproved of the president's policies were Central America and Lebanon.[29] Other polls found comparable results. For example, in August 1983 *The Washington Post* found that 42 percent of its respondents rated Reagan favorably on his handling of foreign affairs in general. However, "his rating was sharply more negative—33 percent approval and 48 percent disapproval—when it came to his handling of problems in El Salvador and Nicaragua. By 54 to 29 percent, those interviewed expressed concern that Reagan is leading the nation more toward war in Central America than away from it."[30]

These declining approval ratings for the administration's policies in Central America and the Middle East indicate that it was not the administration's Soviet policy that needed to be changed in order to win votes. It needed to revamp its approach to Lebanon and Central America. The fact that the White House refused to change its position

28. Barry Sussman, "Criticism of Foreign Policy Growing," *Washington Post,* January 20, 1984; Dennis A. Gilbert, *Compendium of American Public Opinion,* 166. The *Time* poll was conducted by the polling firm Yankelovich, Skelly, and White. Its results were published in Daniel Yankelovich and John Double, "The Public Mood"; and *Time,* January 2, 1984, 31.

29. Gallup found that significantly more people disapproved of the president's policies in Lebanon (52 percent), than approved (34 percent). More people also disapproved of his policies in Central America (44 percent) than approved (36 percent). *Gallup 1983,* 263. See also Page and Shapiro, *Rational Public,* 260.

30. Sussman, "Perceptions," *Washington Post,* August 8, 1983. See also Sussman, "Criticism," *Washington Post,* January 20, 1984.

toward these two regions only underscores that the administration did not develop its foreign policy on the basis of public opinion.

This argument also fails to explain why the White House continued to ardently pursue a superpower rapprochement even after the election had been won. If the Reagan administration had changed its Soviet policy simply to win reelection, there would have been little reason to continue on such a course once the election was over. As soon as the president had secured a second term he would be free to return to his hard-line approach to the Soviet Union, or at least to let the new conciliatory policy languish. This did not happen. In fact, the administration pursued a rapprochement with even greater vigor once the election was over. Immediately after the election results came in the president turned his attention to relations with Moscow. On November 7, 1984—the day after the election—Reagan sent a letter to Soviet General Secretary Konstantin Chernenko. The aim of his note was to induce the Soviet leader to resume arms control talks.[31] Reagan's overture led to a preliminary meeting between Shultz and Foreign Minister Gromyko in January 1985. During the course of that meeting Shultz was able to persuade the Soviets to return to the arms control table. Two months later, Reagan extended an invitation for a summit meeting to the new Soviet leader, Mikhail Gorbachev. Having already won the election, it is unclear why the administration would go to such lengths to improve superpower relations.

In sum, the hypothesis that the Reagan administration changed its Soviet policy in order to win reelection does not adequately explain the catalyst for the policy shift. It assumes that the Reagan administration formed its foreign policy on the basis of public opinion. Such an assumption is unfounded in Reagan's case. Moreover, it was not at all clear that the administration needed to change its Soviet policy in order to attract votes. Some polls suggested that Reagan's popularity had been rising throughout 1983, and that his position vis-à-vis the Democratic presidential candidates had been steadily improving. Support for the administration's Soviet policy had also been increasing. Consequently, there would have been little reason to

31. Oberdorfer, *The Turn*, 97.

reverse course and risk alienating Reagan's conservative supporters. This view also does not explain why the administration continued to pursue a rapprochement once the election was over.

The argument that Reagan reversed his Soviet policy so as to win reelection also fails to satisfy the second criterion for explaining the policy change: it does not adequately explain the timing of the shift. This explanation assumes that because Reagan introduced the new policy at the outset of an election year, the policy shift was part of his reelection campaign. Such assumptions are not proven. There could have been a multitude of reasons for the timing of the president's January 16 address. (In fact, some have even claimed that astrological concerns dictated the timing of Reagan's turning-point address.)[32] Only if all possible reasons for the timing of the speech were considered, and all except the imperatives of the election were found to be wanting, could one accept the argument that U.S. policy was changed so as to strengthen Reagan's reelection prospects. But to argue that the timing demonstrates that the speech was aimed at the election without examining other possible reasons for the timing is unsatisfactory.

Moreover, the issue of timing can be used to argue that the president's address had nothing to do with the election, and everything to do with foreign relations. It would seem logical that if the intent was to attract American voters with his new conciliatory attitude toward the Soviets, the president's speech would have been broadcast during prime television-viewing hours in the United States. This would be the best way to reach a large number of American voters. The Reagan administration did not do this, however. The president's speech was broadcast around the globe at 10 a.m. Washington time, when most Americans were either at work or preparing to go to work. This was 4 p.m. in Western Europe and 6 p.m. in Moscow—perfect timing for evening news broadcasts and the morning editions of newspapers on January 17.

32. The Reagans' astrologer has claimed that she chose the dates and times for the president's major speeches. See Joan Quigley, *What Does Joan Say?: My Seven Years as White House Astrologer to Nancy and Ronald Reagan.*

Furthermore, the administration went to great lengths to attract European and Soviet attention to the speech. A special satellite hookup was used so that the address could be broadcast live to all the U.S. embassies in Europe. Foreign reporters were invited to these embassies to report on the speech as it was being given. The administration also encouraged local television stations in Western Europe to tap into the satellite transmission and to broadcast the address live. The timing of the broadcast and these special arrangements indicate that the Reagan administration was primarily concerned with getting its message across to a foreign audience, not to American voters.[33]

Finally, the domestic politics explanation fails to spell out why U.S. policy changed in the manner it did. It does not explain why the Reagan administration chose to reverse course rather than to simply modify its existing policy. Reagan risked alienating his core group of supporters—conservatives who favored a hard-line approach—by so drastically changing his policy. If it were true that American voters were concerned about Reagan's belligerent rhetoric, why wouldn't the administration simply have toned down its statements, and left it at that? A complete policy reversal seems rather extreme.

This explanation also fails to explain some of the themes that Reagan introduced into U.S. Soviet policy in 1984. As noted in Chapter 2, in January 1984 Reagan officials began asserting that "dangerous misunderstandings" between the superpowers threatened U.S. security. They repeatedly referred to the perils of superpower "miscalculations." It is unclear, however, how the introduction of such a theme would translate into more votes. The sense of urgency surrounding the administration's calls for superpower dialogue also remains unexplained. If the president was simply trying to appeal to moderate voters he could have just called for more dialogue between the two nations. He did not need to repeatedly insist that there was an "imperative" need for dialogue. Nor did he need to invite Gorbachev to a summit meeting long after the election had been won.

33. William E. Farrell, "Reagan Used USIA's Global TV Network," *New York Times,* January 17, 1984.

Moreover, it is not clear how the administration's assertions that it "posed no threat" to the Soviet Union would translate into more votes. Perhaps officials were merely trying to calm Americans' growing concern over a perceived drift toward war. However, if this were the case, these comments would have been addressed to the American people, and phrased in terms of pledges not to initiate conflict with Moscow. Such was not the case. Officials addressed these remarks to the Soviets, and often made them privately, away from public ears. For instance, in the spring of 1984 Reagan wrote a personal letter to General Secretary Chernenko in an effort to allay the "genuine fears" of "some people in the Soviet Union" that the United States meant them harm. That autumn he also arranged a private tête-à-tête with Foreign Minister Gromyko in order to "make it clear that we have no hostile intentions toward his country." In short, the administration's remarks were aimed at the Soviets much more than at American voters.[34]

In conclusion, available evidence suggests that the Reagan administration did not change its Soviet policy in response to the impending 1984 presidential election. This explanation fails to uncover the catalyst for the policy shift; it does not explain the timing of the change; and it does not explain why U.S. policy changed in the manner it did. The following chapter will therefore consider the possibility that George Shultz and Robert McFarlane brought about the change.

---

34. Reagan, An American Life, 595–96; Gwertzman, "Gromyko Meetings End with Accord," New York Times, September 30, 1984.

4

The Passive President

Reagan's Advisers and the Change in U.S. Soviet Policy

> The description of Ike as out of the loop in his own presidency was unquestioned at the time that Eisenhower left office. . . . Today, whether or not presidency scholars approve of Eisenhower's politics, they no longer hold that he was out to lunch. . . . Eisenhower is now recognized to have been, in his own way, very much an activist president.[1]

I N FEBRUARY 1984 COLUMNIST Meg Greenfield queried, "How does Reagan decide?" Although the president was entering his third year in office, little was known about how policy was formulated in his administration. Where did he get his information? With whom did he discuss policy options? On what basis did he evaluate each option? Greenfield thought it "most remarkable" that there was so little interest in Reagan's decision making. "In Washington," she pointed out, "the decision making process, as it is reverently known, is usually an absolute fixation." This lack of interest, Greenfield surmised, had a very simple explanation: most people didn't think of the president as making decisions at all. Decisions were made around Reagan; they did not emanate from him.[2]

1. Fred I. Greenstein, "Ronald Reagan—Another Hidden-Hand Ike?" 7.
2. Meg Greenfield, "How Does Reagan Decide?" *Washington Post*, February 15, 1984.

Historically, American presidents have been the "sole organ," or the preeminent authority, in the determination of U.S. foreign policy.[3] Despite this, many charged that President Reagan was only marginally involved in foreign policy making during his time in office. The president established the broad outlines of U.S. policy, these critics argued, such as the need to strengthen military capabilities and to contain communism, but it was largely up to his senior officials to establish more specific policy goals.

Observers offered several explanations for why the president did not engage in foreign policy making. One view was that Reagan was simply too naive about international affairs to formulate U.S. policy. Periodic comments by unnamed "senior White House officials" on the president's "serious intellectual shortcomings" and his "allergy to detail" upheld this notion of an ignorant president. Reagan's own comments often contributed to this image. For instance, three weeks before the 1985 Geneva summit meeting, the president asserted that there was no word in Russian for "freedom." This inaccuracy was especially disconcerting because Reagan had been studying Soviet politics and culture for months in order to prepare himself for the Geneva meeting. His grasp of arms control issues was particularly tenuous. In the fall of 1983 Reagan stunned members of congress with his admission that he had never realized that most of the Soviet Union's intermediate range nuclear missiles were land-based. Only then, he stated, did he understand why they had called his 1982 proposal to cut all land-based weapons by half "unfair" and "non-negotiable." On another occasion, the president "forgot" that U.S. strategic bombers and cruise missiles were armed with nuclear weapons.[4]

Others suggest that Reagan's detachment from foreign policy making stemmed from lack of interest. It wasn't that he didn't understand international issues; he just didn't care much. Reagan's entire political career had been devoted to domestic politics. As a spokesman for

3. *United States v Curtiss-Wright Export Corporation*, 299 US 304 (1936).

4. Leslie Gelb, "The Mind of the President"; Jane Mayer and Doyle McManus, *Landslide: The Unmaking of the President*, 159; "Six Experts on Soviets Give Reagan Briefing," *New York Times*, November 8, 1985; Don Oberdorfer, "The U.S.-Soviet War of Words Escalates," *Washington Post*, November 21, 1983; Lou Cannon, "Dealings with the Soviets Raise Uncomfortable Questions," *Washington Post*, July 2, 1984.

General Electric in the 1950s, he had toured the country speaking about the evils of big government and heavy taxation. As governor of California, Reagan had focused on cutting the state budget and on streamlining social service programs.[5] His presidential campaigns had also centered around domestic reform. Tax reduction, spending cuts, and economic deregulation formed the main planks of his platform, while his ideas on foreign policy were limited to anticommunism and a pledge to fortify U.S. military capabilities. Upon taking office in 1981 the Reagan administration focused intently on reviving the economy. Consequently, foreign policy took a back seat. "[I]n the first days of the administration [Reagan officials] appeared to believe that foreign policy did not matter much," Secretary of State Alexander Haig complained. "The problems of the nation were essentially domestic and if the economy was made healthy and the government trimmed down, all else would follow naturally."[6]

It was also argued that Reagan's management style left him disconnected from foreign policy making. Upon taking office the president instituted what he called a "cabinet-style" method of decision making. As he described it,

> Instead of the traditional Cabinet meeting with each Cabinet member making a brief report on how things were going in his agency, I wanted this operation where I have the benefit of the thinking of all of them, because most problems do overlap. . . . And so, what we have is an agenda, and it goes out on the table and there have been numerous differences. And . . . when there's been enough discussion and argument, and I've joined in and I've heard enough, I make the decision. . . .[7]

In order for such a decision-making process to work effectively, however, the chief executive must state his final policy decisions clearly,

5. Reagan, *My Early Life, or Where's the Rest of Me?* 251–73.

6. Alexander Haig, *Caveat: Realism, Reagan, and Foreign Policy,* 357.

7. Reagan, Remarks at Rancho de Cielo, California, August 13, 1981, *WCPD* 17:876. For more on the structure of policy making in the Reagan administration, see Frederic A. Waldstein, "Cabinet Government: The Reagan Management Model," 54–75; and Michael Turner, "The Reagan White House, the Cabinet, and the Bureaucracy," 39–67.

so that subordinates may carry them out. Reagan often failed to do this; he rarely gave his subordinates clearly defined tasks. Ronald Reagan may have been "The Great Communicator" to the American public, but behind closed doors he tended to be more nebulous. Referring to the president's elusiveness, former Secretary of the Treasury Donald Regan called Reagan's first term the "guesswork presidency." "Never has [the president] or anyone else, sat down in private to explain to me what is expected of me, what goals he would like to see me accomplish, what results he wants," Regan lamented in early 1981. "I am flying by the seat of my pants." Eventually the treasury secretary decided that he was "free to interpret [the president's] words and implement his intentions . . . according to my best judgement."[8]

Another feature of this management style was the broad delegation of duties. "I don't believe a chief executive should supervise every detail of what goes on in his organization," Reagan has remarked. "The chief executive should set broad policy and general ground rules [and] then let [subordinates] do it. . . . As long as they are doing what you have in mind, don't interfere." Some charged, however, that Reagan had taken this too far. The president often delegated away his own authority to establish policy goals. Journalists Jane Mayer and Doyle McManus argued that the president "did not delegate in the usual sense. He did not actively manage his staff by assigning tasks and insisting on regular progress reports. Instead he typically gave his subordinates little or no direction. Usually, he provided the broad rhetoric and left them to infer what he wanted." Fred I. Greenstein has referred to such practices as the "no hands presidency." Through the excessive delegation of duties and a passive management style, Reagan "remained disconnected from the day-to-day politics and policy."[9]

Some charged that this problem with unclear policy goals and overreliance on subordinates was especially severe in regard to foreign policy making. Calling Reagan "The Great Delegator," Lou Cannon of

8. Donald Regan, *For the Record: From Wall Street to Washington*, chapter 8, and pp. 161 and 159.

9. Reagan, *An American Life*, 161; Mayer and McManus, *Landslide*, 27; Greenstein, "Another Hidden-Hand Ike?" 7, 12.

the *Washington Post* argued that the president's proclivity for allowing subordinates to make basic policy decisions had resulted in a confused and ineffective policy toward the Soviet Union.[10] Haig's account of his days in the Reagan administration supports Cannon's assertion. "[T]here was no description of duty, no rules, no expression of the essential authority of the president to guide his subordinates in their task," Haig asserted.

> In the absence of such a charter there can be no other result than confusion. . . . Not knowing his methods, not understanding his system of thought . . . I had to proceed on the assumption that our principles and our instincts were roughly the same, and that the integrated framework of policy that I advocated would there-fore be acceptable to him. . . . But to me, the White House was as mysterious as a ghost ship; you heard the creak of the rigging and the groan of the timbers and sometimes even glimpsed the crew on deck. But which of the crew had the helm? . . . It was impossible to know for sure.[11]

The situation did not appear to be all that different once George Shultz became secretary of state and Robert McFarlane national se-curity adviser. For instance, during the final months of the 1984 presidential campaign, Shultz and McFarlane put together an agenda of twelve possible policy options for the administration to pursue in the next term. These proposals included the establishment of a new nuclear nonproliferation regime, efforts to revive the West European economies, an expansion of aid to the Third World, and new programs to combat terrorism. Days after the election McFarlane presented this agenda to Reagan. Since all twelve proposals would entail a major investment of the president's time, he was invited to select two or three initiatives for the administration to focus on. The president perused the proposals for several days before giving McFarlane his response. His only comment—"Let's do them all!"[12]

10. Lou Cannon, "Where Delegating Goes Awry," *Washington Post*, May 13, 1985.
11. Haig, *Caveat*, 355–56, 85.
12. David Hoffman, "Reagan to Get Agenda on Foreign Policy," *Washington Post*, November 10, 1984; Mayer and McManus, *Landslide*, 19–20.

In sum, many argued that President Reagan was not a driving force in the formulation of U.S. foreign policy. From this belief follows the assumption that Reagan had little to do with the change in the administration's approach to Moscow. It is assumed that high-level officials in the administration were responsible for the policy change. More specifically, many assume that Secretary of State George Shultz and National Security Adviser Robert McFarlane brought about the more conciliatory policy.[13] Both men, it is pointed out, favored a more forthcoming approach to the Soviet Union. This view differed considerably from their predecessors', and from a majority of the Reagan administration officials, for that matter. Shultz tended to see the Soviet Union more as a rival superpower than as an ideological nemesis. He believed that nonideological factors influenced Soviet behavior, such as its experiences during World War II. The secretary concurred with his colleagues that detente had allowed the Soviet Union to grow stronger at the West's expense, and that a military buildup was therefore necessary. However, he firmly believed that such a buildup should be accompanied by efforts to reduce the tension in the superpower relationship. Toward this end, Shultz advocated an intensified dialogue with Moscow. He also favored a dual track approach to arms control. He maintained that it was necessary for the United States to deploy its intermediate range missiles in Western Europe in order to counterbalance the Soviet SS-20s that threatened the region. But Shultz also felt that these deployments could create daunting political problems for the West European governments because they were facing growing peace movements at the time. Therefore, the secretary argued that deployments should be accompanied by renewed efforts at arms control, and more flexible bargaining positions.[14]

Robert ("Bud") McFarlane shared many of Shultz's views. According to aides at the NSC, the national security adviser and the secretary of state agreed "about eighty percent of the time" on U.S. Soviet

13. For example, see Mandelbaum and Talbott, *Reagan and Gorbachev;* Alexander Dallin and Gail Lapidus, "Reagan and the Russians: American Policy toward the Soviet Union"; Mayer and McManus, *Landslide,* 158; Cannon, *President Reagan,* 509–10; and Oberdorfer, *The Turn,* 70–72.

14. Shultz, *Turmoil and Triumph,* 117–19.

policy. "Bud has a very conservative outlook," Under Secretary of State Lawrence Eagleburger once commented, "but he lets pragmatism get the better of him."[15] While McFarlane believed that the United States should rebuild its military capabilities, he also felt that the president should leave behind a more enduring legacy than simply a military buildup. Reagan should seek to negotiate treaties and agreements with the Soviets that would endure after the president had departed office. Toward this end, McFarlane felt the administration should soften its rhetoric and begin to pursue personal contacts on a broad range of issues. He also emphasized the utility of summit meetings in reducing tensions between the superpowers and, like Shultz, advocated a more flexible position on arms control.[16]

Those who believe that Shultz and McFarlane were responsible for the policy change also point out that these two men were not part of Reagan's original inner circle of foreign policy making (see Table 3). Both assumed their posts shortly before Reagan reversed course. Shultz became secretary of state in June 1982, after personality disputes and policy conflicts forced Alexander Haig to resign. McFarlane succeeded William Clark in October 1983, after Clark became secretary of the interior. Given the lack of presidential authority in foreign policy making, some argue, Shultz and McFarlane simply used their new-found power to shift U.S. policy in a direction more to their liking.

At first glance, this explanation of the change in U.S. policy toward the Soviet Union seems plausible. After President Reagan's performance during the Tower Board hearings, in which he failed to remember various events surrounding the Iran-contra affair, and mistakenly read a private memo from his staff out loud, it is easy to believe that he was not in command of foreign policy making. Likewise, given their views, it seems reasonable that Shultz and McFarlane were responsible

15. Leslie H. Gelb, "Taking Charge: The Rising Power of National Security Adviser Robert McFarlane," 25, 31.

16. McFarlane interview, July 7, 1995. See also McFarlane's memoirs, *Special Trust;* Gelb, "Taking Charge"; and Steven R. Weisman, "The McFarlane Choice," *New York Times,* October 18, 1983.

for the shift in approach to the USSR. However, closer inspection reveals that this bureaucratic advocacy explanation has numerous weaknesses.

The most glaring flaw is that this argument rests entirely upon the assumption that the president had no role in the development of U.S. Soviet policy. Such an assumption is unproven and disregards Reagan's longstanding views on, and fascination with, Soviet communism.

There is clear evidence that Reagan was capable of playing an active role in the development of U.S. foreign policy. However, he picked his spots. As a general rule, the president was not as interested in foreign

Table 3
Turnover in Foreign Policy-Related Positions

Vice President
George H. W. Bush — January 1981 through End of Presidency (EoP)

Secretary of State
Alexander M. Haig Jr. — January 1981
George P. Shultz — July 1982 through EoP

Secretary of Defense
Caspar W. Weinberger — January 1981
Frank Carlucci — November 1987 through EoP

Director of Central Intelligence
William Casey — January 1981–December 1987*
William Webster — May 1988 through EoP

National Security Adviser
Richard Allen — January 1981
William Clark — January 1982
Robert McFarlane — October 1983
John Poindexter — December 1985
Frank Carlucci — January 1987
Colin Powell — November 1987 through EoP

* Robert Gates served as Acting Director of Central Intelligence in the interim.

affairs as he was in domestic issues. Nevertheless, certain foreign issues were very important to him, and he took an active interest in them.

The Strategic Defense Initiative is probably the most widely recognized example of the president's ability to take the initiative in foreign policy development. Few dispute the fact that "Star Wars," as it came to be known, was the president's baby. Reagan first became fascinated with the idea of a defense against nuclear attack in 1979 when he toured the nuclear warning facilities at the North American Aerospace Defense Command (NORAD) in Colorado. NORAD is responsible for detecting any nuclear missiles launched from the Soviet Union, and for providing the president with the information he would need in order to decide whether to launch a retaliatory attack. After viewing the labyrinth of computers and video screens at the facility, Reagan asked Air Force General James Hill what could be done once an incoming missile was detected. Nothing, the general responded. The officials in the target city would have ten or fifteen minutes to take action, but, "That's all we can do. We can't stop it." Reagan was reportedly in disbelief. "We have spent all that money and have all that equipment, and there is nothing we can do to prevent a nuclear missile from hitting us," he commented. "The only options we would have would be to press the button or do nothing. They're both bad. We should have some way of defending ourselves against nuclear missiles."[17]

Believing that the idea of a missile defense system was too controversial to be included in his presidential campaign, Reagan put the idea on the back burner. Upon entering the White House, however, he established a small coterie to examine the possibilities of such a missile defense program. The group operated in extreme secrecy, excluding not only the national security bureaucracy, but top-level advisers as well. The president did not consult Secretary of State Shultz about SDI's ramifications on existing policy, nor did he consult Defense Secretary Weinberger as to its compliance with existing arms

17. On Reagan's role in the development of SDI, see Shultz, *Turmoil and Triumph*, 246–64; Caspar W. Weinberger, *Fighting for Peace: Seven Critical Years in the Pentagon*, 291–329; Karsten Zimmerman, "Decision in March: The Genesis of the 'Star Wars' Speech," 143–58; and Martin Anderson, *Revolution*, 80–99.

treaties. Neither did he confer with the NATO allies. Indeed, even after Reagan publicly unveiled SDI, it remained a closely guarded program. In fact, Shultz was once denied a Pentagon briefing on SDI because he did not have the proper clearance. "It was a very personal project," the secretary acknowledged. "It was very much driven by Ronald Reagan."[18]

Reagan strongly believed in the ability of American scientists to develop a defensive system against nuclear attack. And he supported SDI tenaciously, even in the face of opposition. For example, many scientists doubted that the shield was technically achievable. Defense experts opposed it on the grounds that it would render the world more dangerous by upsetting the doctrine of Mutual Assured Destruction.[19] Politicians and citizens alike warned that SDI would initiate a new arms race in space. Many of Reagan's own advisers were skeptical about the program. Although the president believed that SDI would make nuclear weapons obsolete by protecting Americans from such an attack, others within the administration doubted that SDI was feasible, and therefore felt it was best used as a bargaining chip against the Soviets. Washington should first use the program to threaten Moscow with American technological prowess, and then it should abandon SDI in exchange for large concessions from the Kremlin. Reagan persistently refused to use SDI as such a

18. Shultz made these remarks at a conference on the end of the cold war at Princeton University in February 1993. For accounts of the conference, see Paul Lewis, "Views from the Cold War's Trenches: Ex-Foes Trade Stories," *New York Times,* March 1, 1993. Counselor to the President Ed Meese, National Security Adviser Richard Allen, and the president's science adviser, George Keyworth, were the original key players in the SDI group.

19. Mutual Assured Destruction (MAD) had been the strategic doctrine guiding superpower relations for decades. Basically, it asserts that the way to maintain peace in a bipolar nuclear world is for both sides to have enough nuclear weapons so as to be able to withstand a first strike and still have the capability to launch a retaliatory strike against the initiator. The knowledge that the other side has the capability to retaliate would prevent one from initiating a nuclear attack. Theoretically, the Strategic Defense Initiative would have upset this balance because it could defend one side against a retaliatory second strike, thus eliminating the primary deterrent to initiating a first strike. For an excellent analysis of SDI's destabilizing effects, see Charles Glaser, "Why Even Good Defenses May Be Bad."

negotiating weapon, insisting that his program would make the world safer.[20]

The Iran-contra affair is another example of Reagan's ability to play a decisive role in the development of U.S. foreign policy. Although the administration had initially asserted that the president was on the periphery of the affair, it is now clear that Reagan initiated the misguided policy. His concern for U.S. hostages in Lebanon drove the plan to sell American arms to Iran in exchange for the hostages' release. And it was the president who decided to keep the initiative going even after it became clear the Iranians were not able to free the Americans.[21]

Reagan was also largely responsible for the illegal aid to the contras in Nicaragua. After Congress voted in 1984 to ban further aid to the rebel group, Reagan told McFarlane that he "did not intend to break faith with the contras," signaling that new methods of support had to be found. The following year the president was instrumental in persuading King Fahd of Saudi Arabia to double his contributions to the contras' cause. Reagan mistakenly admitted his responsibility in 1987 when he blurted to a media gathering, "As a matter of fact, I was very definitely involved in the decisions to support the freedom fighters [contra rebels]. It was my idea to begin with."[22]

Reagan continued to press the Iran-contra initiative even after key advisers made their opposition clear. In a crucial meeting on December 7, 1985, Shultz, Weinberger, and Chief of Staff Don Regan all advised the president to abandon the plan. Weinberger spoke for half an hour trying to convince Reagan that "in every way it was a policy that we should not engage in and [which] most likely would not be successful." For once Shultz agreed with Weinberger, arguing that the initiative would "negate our whole policy of not negotiating with

20. McFarlane interview, July 7, 1995. See also Cannon, *President Reagan,* 326.

21. For more detailed accounts of the Iran-contra affair, see Theodore Draper, "Revelations of the North Trial"; and Theodore Draper, *A Very Thin Line: The Iran-Contra Affairs.* See also McFarlane, *Special Trust,* 1–108; and Hedrick Smith, *The Power Game.*

22. Smith, *Power Game,* 620; David Mervin, *Ronald Reagan and the American Presidency,* 158.

terrorists." He also impressed upon the president that the American public would perceive the plan as a strict arms-for-hostages deal, even though Reagan refused to see it that way. At this meeting Don Regan also opposed the operation, arguing that the administration had already invested much without success. Rather than abide by his officials' advice, Reagan proceeded and simply excluded them from the operation.[23]

Evidence regarding the Iran-contra affair does not support the notion that Reagan was a "no hands president." If anything, the portrait that is painted is one of a president who, once focused on an issue, clings to it tenaciously. Discussing the affair, Lou Cannon has observed,

> One side of Reagan's temperament was a passive disengagement from most of the many issues that passed before him. The other side was an intense, almost passionate commitment to causes he visualized in personal terms, as he did the plight of the American hostages. . . . Reagan had both the courage and the ignorance to ignore the collective wisdom of his experts and follow his own counsel when he was convinced he was on the right course.[24]

Likewise, after reviewing the documents from the Oliver North trial, Theodore Draper concluded that Reagan was a "pervasive presence in the contra affair." The papers "show a pattern at glaring variance with the prevailing impression that Reagan had sleepwalked through the contra adventure," Draper remarked. "He was far more the active agent who set the policy and even intervened to implement it."[25]

The Strategic Defense Initiative and the Iran-contra affair both demonstrate that President Reagan was not always the "Great Delegator," as many assert. In both cases he developed and directed U.S. policy. The president formed the policy goals, established advisory

23. Caspar W. Weinberger and George P. Shultz, as quoted in *The Report of the Congressional Committees Investigating the Iran-Contra Affair,* 198. McFarlane's recollection of this meeting confirms these accounts. See McFarlane, *Special Trust,* 46–47.

24. Cannon, *President Reagan,* 630.

25. Draper, "Revelations of the North Trial," 56.

groups to pursue those goals, and took an active interest in guiding the policies to their fruition. These two cases raise another point. In both instances Reagan rejected his officials' advice. Many within the administration felt SDI was a pipe dream and urged the president to bargain it away in order to extract large concessions from the Soviets. Reagan refused. Both Shultz and Weinberger pleaded with the president to abandon his Iran initiative and the illegal support for the contras. Reagan would not. In short, the president did not always take his advisers' counsel. Reagan may not always have been actively involved in the development of foreign policy, but neither was he always the "no hands president." When he had an interest in an issue, Reagan had the capacity to seize control of policy making.

Policy toward the Soviet Union was just such an issue. The Soviet Union was central to Reagan's understanding of international politics. The battle between communism and democracy was the axis upon which international politics turned, he believed. Reagan developed his views about communism and the Soviet Union during his filmmaking days in the 1940s. It was during this period that his Manichaean world-view developed, focusing on the inherent rivalry between democracy and communism. As a leading member of the Screen Actors Guild, Reagan believed that communists were trying to infiltrate Hollywood in an effort to expand their reach. "American movies occupied seventy percent of all the playing time on the world's movie screens in those first years after World War Two," Reagan has recounted, "and, as was to become more and more apparent to me, Joseph Stalin had set out to make Hollywood an instrument of propaganda for his program of Soviet expansionism aimed at communizing the world." From these experiences Reagan concluded that Marxist-Leninist ideology compelled all communist leaders to seek world revolution and the overthrow of democracy.[26]

Reagan's simplistic view of Soviet communists remained rigid for the next forty years. In 1962 Reagan declared that communism was "a single world-wide force dedicated to the destruction of our free enterprise system and the creation of a one-world Socialist state." Six

26. Reagan, *An American Life*, 110.

years later he described Moscow as "the most evil enemy mankind has known in his long climb from the swamp to the stars." "The Soviet Union does not see itself as a status quo power but as a dynamic one," Reagan asserted in 1977, "[it is] interested in the ultimate goal of its philosophic fathers, the global triumph of its political system."[27]

For four decades Reagan had maintained that the Soviet Union was the West's inherent enemy. Accordingly, it is hard to believe that the president would leave the development of policy toward the Soviet Union to others. As political psychologist Betty Glad has noted, one's enemy is highly salient, and "is perceived as actively threatening. . . . He is the source of anxiety and commands our attention and psychological interest." It is implausible that the president would have no interest in his perceived mortal enemy.[28]

Moreover, Reagan's feelings about U.S.-Soviet relations played a role in his decision to seek the presidency. After his failed bid to be the Republican presidential candidate in 1976 Reagan discussed his disappointment with his son, Mike. "You know the real reason I'm upset?" he asked. "I was looking forward to sitting down with Brezhnev and negotiating the SALT II treaty. I wanted to listen to the interpreter tell me for an hour and a half what Brezhnev wanted the president of the United States to give up in order to maintain friendship with Russia. Then I was going to slowly get up, walk around the table and whisper in his ear, 'Nyet.' I'll really miss that."[29]

In sum, there is ample reason to question the assertion that Reagan played a negligible role in the development of policy toward the Soviet Union. Evidence shows that he had the propensity to take control of policy making regarding issues that were of special interest to him. Reagan's deep feelings about communism, and his longstanding belief that the USSR was democracy's nemesis, suggest that superpower relations was just such an issue.

27. See Betty Glad, "Black-and-White Thinking: Ronald Reagan's Approach to Foreign Policy"; Shimko, "Reagan on the Soviet Union," 361; and Reagan, *A Time for Choosing: The Speeches of Ronald Reagan, 1961–1982,* 210.

28. Glad, "Black-and-White Thinking," 36.

29. "Ronald Reagan up Close," *Newsweek,* July 21, 1980, 53.

The hypothesis that Shultz and McFarlane caused U.S. policy to change has another flaw. It requires a great leap in logic. It assumes that because Shultz and McFarlane favored a more conciliatory approach to Moscow, and U.S. policy became more conciliatory, that these two officials *caused* U.S. policy to change. However, in order to make such an argument, one must establish the causal link. One must prove that Shultz and McFarlane took the reins of U.S. foreign policy and redirected it. Such proof is difficult, if not impossible, to establish.

For one thing, Shultz and McFarlane were not the only ones involved in foreign policy making. U.S. policy toward the Soviet Union was developed primarily within the National Security Planning Group (NSPG), an informal body established by the president in August 1981. Besides the president, the key officials in the NSPG were Vice President Bush, Secretary of State Shultz, Secretary of Defense Weinberger, National Security Adviser McFarlane, CIA Director William Casey, and Counselor to the President, Ed Meese.[30]

The NSPG was split down the middle regarding policy toward the Soviet Union. As already noted, Shultz and McFarlane favored a pragmatic approach, and Vice President Bush usually weighed in here as well. This group supported a military buildup, but insisted that such actions should be combined with efforts to engage the Soviet Union in dialogue on a broad range of issues. The negotiation of new arms control agreements was particularly important.

The more conservative faction was led by Defense Secretary Weinberger, and included Meese and Casey. These hard-liners viewed the Soviet Union in ideological terms: Because of its communist ideology, the USSR was inherently expansionist and sought global dominance. Thus, the Soviets sought the demise of the capitalist West. Compromises with Moscow were therefore to be avoided, these hard-liners maintained, because they would be used to further weaken the West.

30. Leslie Gelb, "Foreign Policy System Criticized by U.S. Aides," *New York Times,* October 19, 1981; Bob Woodward, *Veil: The Secret Wars of the CIA,* 180. Chief of Staff James Baker, Deputy Chief of Staff Michael Deaver, and Chairman of the Joint Chiefs of Staff Jack Vessey were also members of the NSPG, although they only played peripheral roles in the formulation of foreign policy. See Michael K. Deaver, *Behind the Scenes.*

The hard-line faction focused on the Soviet Union's military capabilities to the exclusion of almost all else. "In the early 1980s it was apparent that we were lagging," Weinberger has explained. "The Soviets had a dangerous lead and America was running the danger of being seen as a weak and unreliable ally." The United States could not have a strong foreign policy unless it had a strong military. Consequently, Weinberger, Casey, and Meese felt Washington should focus on building up its military capabilities rather than engaging in arms control negotiations. The pursuit of arms control was misguided, they believed, because it furthered the West's relative inferiority. Weinberger and his compadres therefore vehemently opposed Shultz's suggestions that the United States pursue arms talks with the Soviets. "The State Department was uncomfortable with the rebuilding effort and thought arms treaties were the way to go," Weinberger maintains. "There was a tremendous reliance on the arms *process*. State thought the forum for discussion was in and of itself beneficial." The defense secretary and his fellow hard-liners were skeptical of the arms control process because they believed it had allowed the Soviets to gain military superiority. Moreover, they felt such talks would obligate the United States to abandon parts of its rebuilding efforts. "For negotiation to succeed you had to give up something, and we had nothing to give up," Weinberger has contended. "Besides, it is nice to have a good treaty, but no treaty is better than a bad treaty." The hard-liners also asserted that the Soviets habitually abrogated arms control treaties. Therefore, negotiating new ones was futile.[31]

In short, only some of Reagan's top advisers favored a more conciliatory approach to the Soviet Union. If one is to argue that Reagan played a negligible role in policy making, and therefore, that his advisers actually formulated policy, one must explain why the Shultz-McFarlane faction became dominant rather than the more conservative group that had been controlling policy for three years.

But evidence suggests that the Shultz faction was not dominant. The hard-line faction was stronger and had more influence over foreign policy making during late 1983 and early 1984. In order to illustrate this more clearly, each official will be discussed in greater detail.

31. Weinberger interview, July 31, 1995.

Caspar Weinberger

Unlike Shultz and McFarlane, Caspar Weinberger had been Ronald Reagan's longtime friend and political associate. Reagan and Weinberger first met in 1965, and the following year Weinberger assisted Reagan in his first bid for the governorship of California. In 1968 Governor Reagan appointed Weinberger director of finance, where he remained until the end of Reagan's term.

Although Weinberger was not part of Reagan's presidential campaign, he did consult frequently with the candidate about a variety of issues, including U.S. military capabilities. Weinberger privately coveted the position of secretary of state, hoping his friendship with Reagan would afford him such an appointment. The president, however, had different ideas. Immediately after winning the 1980 election, Reagan asked Weinberger to be secretary of defense. Although disappointed, Weinberger accepted the offer, believing that his relationship with the president would allow him to play a more pivotal role in the development of foreign policy than is customary for defense secretaries. This was, in fact, what developed, and both Alexander Haig and George Shultz frequently complained that Weinberger habitually overstepped his authority in the development and implementation of foreign policy.[32]

Despite his aspiration to be secretary of state, Weinberger took the helm of the Defense Department lacking detailed knowledge of military and international affairs. A lawyer by training, his previous political experience had revolved entirely around domestic and budgetary issues. This lack of practical experience caused him to fall back on an ideological approach to U.S.-Soviet relations. It also caused him to rely heavily on subordinates for advice. Foremost among these advisers was Richard Perle, assistant secretary for international security policy. A Washington insider with a great interest in arms control negotiations, Perle had a "passionate distrust of the Soviet Union" and "an unshakable belief that the Soviets had always managed to bend arms control agreements to their advantage and always would."

32. Weinberger, *Fighting for Peace*, 9–15; Cannon, *President Reagan*, 84, 302.

Consequently, Perle tended to reinforce Weinberger's own ideological antipathy for the USSR.[33]

As head of the largest department in the federal government, Weinberger commanded more influence than perhaps any other Cabinet official. Moreover, the administration's military buildup gave him added prestige. As secretary of defense, Weinberger oversaw the largest peacetime military buildup in the nation's history and in 1982 commanded a $219 billion budget. The buildup also meant that it was not in Weinberger's institutional interests to foster improvements in the superpower relationship. Any easing in the tension between the United States and the USSR ran the risk of undermining public support for increased defense expenditures. If Weinberger's budget was reduced, his power might diminish as well. Consequently, the defense secretary emphasized the threat posed by the Soviet Union's military superiority. He argued that any new arms control agreement would further weaken the United States, and asserted that the United States should not abide by the limitations established in the SALT II treaty. Weinberger also opposed Secretary Shultz's 1982 proposal for a Reagan-Andropov summit meeting, and did not support the 1985 meeting between Reagan and Gorbachev in Geneva. Weinberger "is the ultimate advocate," Lou Cannon once observed, "—a shrewd, articulate, and extremely stubborn lawyer who uses his legal skills to champion whatever client he represents at the moment." And during the Reagan presidency, Weinberger's client was the U.S. military.[34]

33. During the 1950s Caspar Weinberger served as a California state legislator. Under Presidents Nixon and Ford, he had been chairman of the Federal Trade Commission, director of the Office of Management and Budget, and Secretary of Health, Education, and Welfare. See Ronald Brownstein and Nina Easton, *Reagan's Ruling Class: Portraits of the President's Top 100 Officials*, 435–37, 497.

34. Brownstein and Easton, *Reagan's Ruling Class*, 433. Weinberger opposed the Geneva summit because he believed the United States would have to "give away" too much at the meeting. Weinberger was not included in the rather large entourage that accompanied President Reagan to Geneva, but his views were made public when a letter, in which he outlined his reservations about the meeting, was leaked to the major newspapers. See Michael R. Gordon, "Weinberger Urges U.S. to Avoid Vow on 1979 Arms Pact," *New York Times*, November 16, 1985; and Walter Pincus "Avoid SALT II Pledge, Weinberger Bids Reagan," *Washington Post*, November 16, 1985.

Edwin Meese III

Often described as one of Reagan's closest aides, Counselor to the President Ed Meese initially exercised extraordinary power over the development of U.S. Soviet policy. Like Weinberger, he had a long-standing friendship with the president, joining the Reagan camp during the 1960s. Meese started out as the governor's legal affairs secretary, and then served as his chief of staff for six years, until Reagan left the post. In 1980 he became chief of staff of Reagan's presidential campaign. Once the election had been won, Meese directed the transition period.[35]

Although he longed to be the president's chief of staff, Meese was a poor administrator, and was given the post of counselor to the president instead. His mandate was to serve as the administration's chief policy spokesman, and to coordinate all policy making. As such, the counselor served as the main conduit to the president, affording him much influence.[36]

Meese's position as policy coordinator initially allowed him to play a pivotal role in the formulation of foreign policy. Upon entering office Reagan had sought to thwart internal battles over foreign policy making by restricting the role of the national security adviser. The national security adviser reported to Meese rather than to the president directly. Meese considered the national security adviser's proposals, and then decided which ones should be forwarded to the president. Consequently, he wielded significant influence over foreign policy. Meese acquired even more power once it became clear that Secretary of State Haig's abrasive personality would insure him a short tenure in the administration.

Meese's influence over foreign policy was curtailed in 1982 when William Clark became the administration's second national security adviser. Also an old friend of Reagan's, Clark demanded that he

35. Philip Taubman, "At the Pentagon and State Dept.: Pragmatic Tone," *New York Times*, March 2, 1981; Brownstein and Easton, *Reagan's Ruling Class*, 643–45.

36. For more on the judgment that Meese did not have the capabilities to be the White House chief of staff, see Deaver, *Behind the Scenes*, 123–25; Cannon, *President Reagan*, 69–71; and Taubman, "Pragmatic Tone," *New York Times*, March 2, 1981.

be granted direct access to the president. Yet although Meese was removed from the paper flow regarding foreign policy, he did remain an integral member of the National Security Planning Group.[37]

Meese had no prior experience in international affairs and often fell back on his legal training and ideological views in formulating his opinions on U.S.-Soviet relations. As one journalist described him, Meese was "the conservative conscience" of the Reagan administration. He had known Weinberger for decades and tended to side with him on almost all foreign policy issues, including the SALT II treaty. A strong believer in the Strategic Defense Initiative, Meese was a central member of the small group Reagan created to look into nuclear defense after winning the presidency.[38]

William Casey

Unlike Weinberger and Meese, CIA Director Bill Casey was not part of the California clique surrounding Reagan. An affluent New York attorney, Casey had been active in Republican party politics for decades. He first met Reagan in 1979 and a strong friendship quickly developed. Soon after their meeting, Casey became chairman of the "Reagan for President" organization. In 1980, after collecting half a million dollars toward the cause, Casey was appointed Reagan's presidential campaign adviser.[39]

37. It is quite likely that Meese's control over foreign policy making would have been curtailed even without Clark insisting that he have direct access to the president. Many in the White House felt Meese had failed to give foreign policy issues the attention they deserved. This was partly due to the fact that Meese was spread too thin and partly because of his disorganization. (Meese's briefcase had become known within the administration as the "bottomless pit" and the "black hole.") See Gelb, "Foreign Policy System Criticized," New York Times, October 19, 1981; and Deaver, Behind the Scenes, 131–37.

38. Mayer and McManus, Landslide, 31; Smith, Power Game, 585–96; Anderson, Revolution, 80–99. In fact, although the president did not consult with Weinberger on SDI, Meese did let the defense secretary in on the broad outlines of the project. See Weinberger, Fighting for Peace, 305.

39. See Woodward, Veil, 37, 135; and Weinberger, Fighting for Peace, 27.

Unlike the other hard-liners, Casey had prior experience in foreign relations and intelligence gathering. During World War II he had directed economic intelligence for the Office of Strategic Services (OSS). After the war, Casey served as associate general counsel of the Marshall Plan, and played a role in the birth of the Central Intelligence Agency. During the 1970s he was under secretary of state for economic affairs, and a member of the President's Foreign Intelligence Advisory Board.[40]

Like Weinberger, Casey sought to be secretary of state. However, Reagan supporters felt he did not have a strong enough background in international affairs to compensate for the president's lack of experience, and offered Casey the directorship of the CIA instead. Wanting more of a role in policy formulation, Casey made it clear that he would only accept the position if it was given Cabinet ranking. This was granted, and Casey gained more power over foreign policy making than any of his predecessors. As Bob Woodward noted, the Director of Central Intelligence became "the shadow secretary of state," which resulted in much acrimony between the CIA and the State Department.[41]

Casey firmly aligned himself in the Weinberger-Meese camp regarding U.S.-Soviet relations. Doubting the Soviets' trustworthiness, he opposed new arms control agreements and felt the administration should not honor the limits established by the SALT II treaty. Accordingly, the CIA produced a never-ending stream of reports to the president regarding the Soviet arms buildup and treaty violations. Casey was also concerned about U.S. technology leaking to the Soviets, and as a remedy he advocated restrictions on exports of scientific knowledge.[42]

Critics charged that Casey used his position as DCI to promote his own agenda. In 1981 Leslie Gelb observed in *The New York Times* that Casey "reaches well beyond the role of simply providing intelligence estimates, and offers recommendations on a wide range of policy

40. Brownstein and Easton, *Reagan's Ruling Class*, 612–14.
41. Woodward, *Veil*, 490–97.
42. Smith, *Power Game*, 585–92; Woodward, *Veil*, 101, 489; Brownstein and Easton, *Reagan's Ruling Class*, 613.

issues. . . . Mr. Meese called him 'virtually a full partner' " in foreign policy making. This arrangement was roundly criticized by those who believed that the CIA should be in the business of providing objective information, rather than making policy. Casey "had an agenda as big as 'a house," one official confided, and he used intelligence information so as to bolster his own policy positions. Those within the agency complained that they were pressured to "toe the party line" with their assessments. Reports that did not conform with Casey's views did not reach the Oval Office. Secretary Shultz complained, "The CIA and Bill Casey were as independent as a hog on ice and could be as confident as they were wrong." Consequently, Shultz frequently questioned the credibility of Casey's intelligence assessments.[43]

George P. Shultz

In contrast to Weinberger, Meese, and Casey, George Shultz had only met Ronald Reagan a few times before joining his administration in 1982. Although he lived in Stanford, he was not part of Reagan's California clique.

Before becoming the sixtieth secretary of state, Shultz had had little experience in international politics. A labor economist by training, he had spent twenty years in academia, working intermittently as a labor mediator. Although he held three Cabinet posts during the Nixon administration, all revolved around finance and labor negotiation. None afforded him much experience in the formulation of foreign policy. Consequently, Shultz did not come to office with a foreign policy agenda of his own. Moreover, he was appointed to his post so suddenly that he did not have time to establish an agenda before

---

43. Gelb, "Foreign Policy System Criticized," *New York Times,* October 19, 1981. Author interview with anonymous official; Melvin Goodman, former Senior Analyst in the Division of Soviet Affairs, The Central Intelligence Agency, during Roundtable on the Role of Intelligence, annual meeting of the International Society for Political Psychology, Washington, D.C., July 8, 1995. In Goodman's view, the politicization of the CIA was one of the main reasons the agency failed to predict the dissolution of the USSR. See also Les Aspin, "Misreading Intelligence," 166–72. Shultz, *Turmoil and Triumph,* 84, 490, 691.

taking over. In 1982 Shultz was president of the Bechtel Corporation, a huge California-based construction firm. On June 25 Shultz was in the middle of a meeting in London when the president contacted him about the appointment. Reagan explained that Alexander Haig had just resigned, and that he wanted to announce Haig's successor at the same time he announced the resignation. Shultz had to decide at that moment. By the next morning Shultz had resigned from Bechtel and was on his way to Washington to prepare for his nomination hearings.[44]

Unlike his predecessor, Shultz was acutely aware that historical precedent established the president as the primary force in U.S. foreign policy. He believed that the secretary of state should have no foreign policy of his own, only that of the president. Consequently, he was extremely reticent about his own policy views while in office. Even those close to him professed ignorance as to where he stood on specific issues in U.S.-Soviet relations, and his aides at the State Department described him as being "Buddhalike."[45]

Shultz was rather deferential and emphasized his secondary status. "Unlike Mr. Haig, [Shultz] does not push those positions that are contrary to what he thinks are presidential inclinations," reads one typical commentary on the secretary. "Unlike Mr. Haig, he subordinates himself at every opportunity to Mr. Reagan." His favorite metaphor for his job was that of a "gardener of diplomacy," one who persistently cultivates the soil of relations for some future bounty to be reaped by others. When asked about the success of his diplomatic trips abroad Shultz typically responded to reporters, "Oh, you know . . . I am just secretary of state. My trips aren't successful. I just talk to people."[46]

44. See Shultz, *Turmoil and Triumph,* 3–15, 27–29, 117–19; and Don Oberdorfer, "Man behind the Mask," *Washington Post,* February 3, 1986.
45. Leslie H. Gelb, "Shultz after a Year in Office: Looking for Success Abroad," *New York Times,* August 1, 1983; Bernard Gwertzman, "The Shultz Method: How the New Secretary of State Is Trying to Stabilize Foreign Policy," 15, 28.
46. Gelb, "Shultz after a Year," *New York Times,* August 1, 1983; Oberdorfer, "Man behind the Mask," *Washington Post,* February 3, 1986; Bernard Gwertzman, "No Headlines, No Fanfare: This is Shultz," *New York Times,* May 17, 1985.

Unlike Haig, Shultz eschewed publicity. Virtually all foreign policy announcements were made from the White House rather than from the State Department. By the fall of 1983 Shultz had given only nine speeches and six Washington press conferences. Reporters complained that they could go weeks without hearing from him, while television correspondents at the State Department began to refer to him as the "phantom of the seventh floor." When he did meet with reporters the secretary usually revealed little. He spoke only in broad terms, and often declined to discuss the more noteworthy issues. He also chose his words carefully, so as not to generate headlines.[47]

Shultz took a methodical, incremental approach to the development of foreign policy. Believing that every issue can be seen from various vantage points, and that each view has its own merit, he took much time before forming policy positions. The secretary carefully scrutinized every component of an issue, seeking ways to forge a consensus. Using phrases like "advance the process" and "plan for the long haul," Shultz's style was to move gradually toward the foreign policy goals President Reagan established.[48]

Shultz also saw himself as a team player and preferred a collegial approach to foreign policy formulation. He favored gathering groups of experts and politicians with an interest in specific issues and having roundtable discussions in which each could discuss his views. The secretary often set up teams of experts and asked them to develop competing positions on an issue.[49]

By mid-1983 Shultz's reticence and his plodding, incremental approach to foreign policy had begun to draw criticism. Detractors claimed that the secretary's creeping pace was actually due to his lack of experience. They believed that because he entered office with no agenda of his own, he had to devote much time to developing his

47. Don Oberdorfer, "Disgrace: Shultz's Roar on Policy Making Got Results," *Washington Post,* October 23, 1983; Bernard Gwertzman, "Reticence and Foreign Policy," *New York Times,* October 8, 1985; Gwertzman, "No Headlines," *New York Times,* May 17, 1985.

48. Oberdorfer, "Disgrace," *Washington Post,* October 23, 1983; Gwertzman, "The Shultz Method," 32, 15.

49. Gwertzman, "The Shultz Method," 28, 32.

ideas and forming positions. The secretary's focus on proceduralism, some charged, was meant to conceal a lack of substance.[50]

Additionally, unnamed "White House officials" charged in the press that the secretary's demeanor and management style had created a leadership void in foreign policy making. Shultz's emphasis on consensus-building was perceived as excessive timidity. The secretary of state was "too reticent to take control," some charged, and as a result, U.S. policy remained incoherent. "If Shultz is to take a more forceful role," senior officials commented anonymously in *The Washington Post*, "he will have to grasp the reins of leadership in a way that is uncharacteristic for him." Throughout the second half of 1983 there was constant speculation in the press that the secretary might resign because of his inability to play an authoritative role in policy formulation.[51]

Robert C. McFarlane

Robert McFarlane did not know Ronald Reagan when he was promoted to national security adviser on October 16, 1983. Thus, he did not have the immediate rapport with the president that his predecessor and many other administration officials had. However, McFarlane had had much experience in the foreign policy bureaucracy. A former lieutenant colonel in the Marines, he had served on the National Security Council (NSC) staffs under both President Richard Nixon and his successor, Gerald Ford. In 1981 McFarlane had been working as a staff member for the Senate Armed Services Committee when Secretary Haig recruited him to be the State Department counselor.

50. Ibid. There may be some truth to this, as Shultz was much more forthcoming on economic issues, which is his area of expertise. See Gwertzman, "Reticence," *New York Times,* October 8, 1985.

51. John M. Goshko and Michael Getler, "Shultz No Longer Seen as Driving Force in Foreign Policy," *Washington Post,* August 15, 1983; "Disappearing Act at Foggy Bottom," *Time,* August 1, 1983; Oberdorfer, "Disgrace," *Washington Post,* October 23, 1983; Steven R. Weisman, "The Influence of William Clark"; "Why the Shultzes Can't Win," *Newsweek,* August 29, 1983; "Clark Appointment Catches State Department Unawares," *New York Times,* October 14, 1983.

The following year, he moved to the NSC as deputy to the new national security adviser, William Clark. When Clark was appointed secretary of the interior in the fall of 1983, McFarlane replaced him.[52]

Although McFarlane would go on to have much power over foreign policy making, at the time that the administration reversed its Soviet policy, he was still the new kid on the block. McFarlane's colleagues perceived him to be a "quintessential staff man," and a "perennial number two man" who had attained high office fortuitously. A career bureaucrat with no political ambitions of his own, McFarlane had been appointed largely because he did not threaten the current balance of power within the administration.[53]

Moreover, McFarlane's self-effacing style further undermined his initial power. Although he had more foreign policy experience than any of his colleagues, he spoke infrequently at policy making meetings, preferring to listen to others. Like Shultz, he sought to avoid the spotlight. He eschewed the media, granting interviews as rarely as possible, and almost always spoke off the record. According to his staff, McFarlane's working credo was "There is no limit to what a man can do or where he can go if he doesn't mind who gets the credit."[54]

McFarlane was appointed national security adviser during a tumultuous period in U.S. foreign relations, suggesting that he had little time to devote to Soviet policy. Only one week after he took his post, 241 U.S. marines in Beirut were killed by a terrorist bombing. Just two days later the United States invaded Grenada. Moreover, McFarlane was

52. See Steven R. Weisman, "Reagan and Aides Said to Dispute Clark's Successor," *New York Times,* October 15, 1983. It should also be noted that Shultz did not necessarily perceive McFarlane to be an ally within the administration. See Shultz, *Turmoil and Triumph,* 490, 503, 509, and 511, among other references.

53. Weisman, "Reagan and Aides," *New York Times,* October 15, 1983; Steven R. Weisman, "Reagan Delaying on Security Aide," *New York Times,* October 16, 1983; Weisman, "McFarlane Called Choice of Reagan for Security Post," *New York Times,* October 17, 1983; William E. Farrell, "McFarlane Named Security Adviser by the President," *New York Times,* October 18, 1983; Steven R. Weisman, "The McFarlane Choice"; John M. Goshko, " 'Mistake': Kirkpatrick Thought Clark Should Stay," *Washington Post,* October 23, 1983.

54. Leslie Gelb, "Security Council's 'Mr. Indispensable,' " *New York Times,* October 18, 1983; Gelb, "Taking Charge."

continually called upon to mediate policy disputes between Shultz and Weinberger, who rarely saw eye-to-eye. "The most McFarlane can do on the big questions like Soviet affairs," one White House official confided in early 1984, "is set up temporary fences between the elephants to keep them, for a few days, from trampling all over one another."[55]

Therefore, in order to argue that Shultz and McFarlane "won" the battle for dominance over U.S. Soviet policy, one must demonstrate that the hard-liners either changed their views, or were defeated. There is no evidence to support the former, and, as demonstrated, Shultz and McFarlane lacked the institutional power to foist their views upon the rest of the administration.[56] Shultz's position was especially precarious in 1983–1984, as was evidenced by repeated criticisms that he had left a leadership void in foreign policy making, and recurrent rumors that he would soon resign. The secretary's lack of foreign policy experience and low-key demeanor also make it difficult to accept that he imposed his policy views on the administration. A deferential man, Shultz viewed himself primarily as a servant to the president. His role was to implement the president's foreign policy agenda, not to pursue his own. Moreover, one must keep in mind that Shultz did not seek dramatic changes in U.S. policy. That was not his style. Rather, he sought slow, incremental improvements in East-West relations. The fact that the administration abruptly reversed course in 1984 suggests that Shultz was not the impetus for the change.

It is also important to note that the president did not always accept Shultz's advice regarding U.S.-Soviet relations. For instance, when General Secretary Brezhnev died in November 1982, Shultz argued strongly that the president should attend the funeral and use the opportunity to meet incoming leader Yuri Andropov. Reagan refused,

55. Leslie H. Gelb, "McFarlane Carving His Niche," New York Times, March 28, 1984.

56. Caspar Weinberger remained opposed to the more conciliatory approach through 1987 when he resigned as secretary of defense. See Weinberger, Fighting for Peace; Lou Cannon, "Reagan Voices Summit Hopes," New York Times, November 17, 1985; and Cannon, President Reagan, 749–50.

sending Shultz and Vice President Bush instead. In March of the following year the secretary proposed that Washington should slowly begin to pursue dialogue with the Kremlin on a broad range of issues. Reagan responded by giving his infamous "evil empire" speech, and allowing the proposal to languish, effectively overruling it. An integral part of Shultz's proposal was a meeting between himself, Soviet Foreign Minister Gromyko, and General Secretary Andropov in Moscow during July. Shultz hoped to use the meeting to lay the groundwork for a possible Reagan-Andropov summit meeting in 1984. However, as July approached, Reagan nixed Shultz's visit, asserting that Soviet behavior remained intransient. (This incident is especially interesting. It is curious that Reagan would repudiate Shultz's efforts to improve U.S.-Soviet relations in the summer of 1983, yet reverse himself and adopt a more conciliatory stance five months later. Moreover, Reagan's reversal came after the Soviets had shot down KAL flight 007.) In short, Reagan vetoed Shultz's proposals regarding superpower relations with some regularity. This suggests that he would not blindly follow the secretary down a path the president himself did not want to take.[57]

McFarlane's appointment to national security adviser probably strengthened Shultz's position within the administration somewhat. McFarlane's predecessor, William Clark, had been a conservative ideologue and had frequently clashed with Shultz over policy recommendations. Thus, Clark's removal alone probably boosted Shultz's standing slightly. However, although Shultz and McFarlane shared similar views regarding foreign policy, the two men were not especially close. Shultz had disapproved of the way McFarlane had handled his previous assignment as special envoy to the Middle East, and had felt that McFarlane was not the best person to succeed Clark. For his part, McFarlane grew weary of mediating the constant disputes between Shultz and Weinberger. Moreover, Shultz's institutional weakness continued well into 1984, suggesting that McFarlane's

57. Oberdorfer, "War of Words," *Washington Post,* November 21, 1983; Shultz, *Turmoil and Triumph,* 265; Oberdorfer, *The Turn,* 40, 43–45; Cannon, *President Reagan,* 311; Leslie H. Gelb, "Expanding Contacts with Soviets," *New York Times,* June 30, 1983.

appointment did not give him the additional strength that some have suggested.[58]

In contrast, the hard-line faction was quite strong in late 1983 and early 1984. Weinberger, Meese, and Casey had known the president far longer than had Shultz and McFarlane. Thus, they had greater access to him, and thus, more influence over him. These hard-liners had also developed strong relationships among themselves, and were therefore able to coordinate their policy positions, thus presenting a united front. Moreover, unlike Shultz and McFarlane, the hard-liners had been in command of foreign policy making since the administration had taken office. They had had years to establish their bureaucratic strength, foster political ties, and institutionalize their views.

All this would indicate that the hard-line faction should have had much power and influence over the development of U.S. Soviet policy in late 1983 and early 1984. In fact, it did. This is demonstrated by the conservative nature of U.S. Soviet policy between 1981 and the end of 1983. It is also demonstrated by another incident which occurred in October 1983, only two months before the new policy was announced. Weary of all the fighting within the administration, in October 1983 National Security Adviser William Clark asked the president to assign him to a more congenial post. Reagan complied with his old friend's wish, and on October 13 took Washington by surprise by naming Clark as the successor to outgoing Secretary of the Interior James G. Watt. Looking for a change themselves, Chief of Staff James Baker and Deputy Chief of Staff Michael Deaver proposed that Baker become the new national security adviser with Deaver then succeeding him as chief of staff. Reagan quickly accepted this arrangement, believing it would be less disruptive than leaving the post open and conducting a lengthy search for a successor. The president planned to inform his top advisers of his decision at the NSPG meeting on October 14, and to then announce it to the press immediately afterward. However, the hard-liners got wind of the job switch just before the NSPG meeting and immediately organized a revolt. Weinberger, Casey, and Meese all opposed Jim Baker taking the helm at the National Security Council. It

58. Shultz, *Turmoil and Triumph*, 318–20.

would be disastrous, they argued, to have such a moderate formulating U.S. Soviet policy. "One of their principal arguments," comments Lou Cannon, "was that the selection of Baker as national security adviser would send a signal of accommodation to the Soviets. This was a . . . potent argument in the fall of 1983, when memories of KAL 007 were still fresh. . . ." Casey in particular was horrified by the prospect, calling it "intolerable," and pressing instead for the appointment of Jeanne Kirkpatrick, U.S. ambassador to the United Nations.[59]

Faced with three of his top officials on the verge of resignation, Reagan decided to postpone his press announcement. Seeing the discord his proposal had brought, and knowing the hard-liners' antagonism would only grow if he assumed the post at the NSC, Baker suggested to Reagan that he scrap the plan. Relieved, Reagan consented. After much more wrangling in which the hard-liners rallied around the hawkish Kirkpatrick, Reagan ultimately chose a compromise candidate in Robert McFarlane.

Thus, in mid-October 1983 the hard-liners within the Reagan administration were powerful enough to block Jim Baker's appointment to the NSC. The main reason for their opposition was Baker's more moderate views on superpower relations. It is curious that the Weinberger faction would be influential enough to block this appointment, but powerless to stop a wholesale reversal in U.S. policy weeks later. Surely, if they were opposed to Baker's nomination on the grounds of his moderate views, they would be opposed to adopting a more conciliatory stance toward the Soviet Union. Why were they not able to stop it? They had longer ties with Reagan; they had been in the administration longer than the more moderate Shultz and McFarlane; they had been able to stop such changes in the past. The hard-liners' inability to block the policy reversal strongly suggests that someone with more authority than themselves established the new direction. The only one with such authority was President Reagan himself.

59. Cannon, *President Reagan*, 431. This account of the plan for Jim Baker to succeed Clark as national security adviser was drawn from various sources. For more detail, see Smith, *Power Game*, 320–24; Woodward, *Veil*, 282–84; Reagan, *An American Life*, 448; Mayer and McManus, *Landslide*, 58–59; Cannon, *President Reagan*, 427–34; and Deaver, *Behind the Scenes*, 129–30, among others.

This raises a final point. George Shultz has never claimed to be the mastermind behind the shift in U.S. policy. This is noteworthy because it would certainly be in his political interests to take credit for a policy that turned out to be so successful. In fact, Shultz has stated repeatedly that he was simply carrying out President Reagan's objectives.[60] The president, Shultz insists, was responsible for the change in U.S. policy toward the Soviet Union.

Reagan's recollections appear to support Shultz's view. In his memoirs, the president insinuates that the secretary was simply his messenger, carrying out Reagan's policy. For example, in November 1983 Reagan reflected in his diary:

> George Shultz and Cap Weinberger are having one of their disputes over policy. Cap is not as interested as George in . . . negotiating with the Russians. . . . Bill Casey and Ed Meese lined up in Cap's camp in favoring an even harder line. . . . The dispute is so out of hand that George sounds like he might want out. I can't let that happen. George is carrying out my policy.[61]

Conclusion

While the argument that Secretary Shultz and National Security Adviser McFarlane brought about the change in U.S. Soviet policy seems reasonable at first glance, closer examination reveals its weaknesses. Most significantly, this bureaucratic politics explanation is unable to explain the catalyst for the policy reversal. It claims that George Shultz and Robert McFarlane caused U.S. policy to shift, yet such an assertion is not convincing. It rests on the assumption that Reagan was a "no hands president" who passively sat by while others ran his administration. It assumes that he delegated away all his authority over foreign policy. However, as was demonstrated in the Iran-contra episode and the Strategic Defense Initiative, Reagan did have the capacity to take charge of foreign policy making.

60. Shultz, *Turmoil and Triumph,* 159–69; Oberdorfer, *The Turn,* 15–17; 34–37.
61. Reagan, *An American Life,* 605–6.

This explanation also requires one to accept that a weaker faction, composed of relative newcomers to foreign policy making, came to overrule an established hard-line faction within the administration. It disregards the relative strength and influence of the hard-liners and neglects the personal and institutional weaknesses of Shultz and McFarlane.

This raises another point. In 1983 the balance of power within the Reagan administration favored the hard-liners. Weinberger and his allies continued to dominate foreign policy making. This suggests that U.S. policy toward the Soviet Union should have remained antagonistic. The hard-liners should have continued to call the shots. At the very least, there should have been a stalemate between the blocs. The shift to a more conciliatory approach suggests that someone with more authority, someone able to overrule these factions, took the reins. The only one with such authority was President Reagan.

This bureaucratic politics argument also does not explain the timing of the policy change. It fails to explain why U.S. Soviet policy changed in January 1984. Shultz joined the administration in June 1982. Why did policy not shift then? One may counter that Shultz was too weak at that point and needed McFarlane's appointment to bolster his standing. However, as discussed, Shultz's position remained weak after McFarlane's appointment. Moreover, at the time of the policy change McFarlane was still new to his position and too bogged down with other concerns to have been able to draw up and push through a policy reversal. Thus, it is doubtful that he precipitated the change.

This explanation also does not clarify why U.S. policy changed in the manner it did. Some of the changes introduced in January 1984 can plausibly be linked to Shultz's and McFarlane's views. For instance, Reagan called for the institutionalization of regular meetings between U.S. and Soviet leaders in his turning-point address. Both Shultz and McFarlane had favored more dialogue. Also, beginning in 1984 Washington took a more active interest in arms control and adopted more negotiable bargaining positions. Shultz and McFarlane had both advocated such an approach. It is also plausible that the secretary was behind the administration's new emphasis on confidence-building measures. Such a nonideological approach was very much in sync with Shultz's penchant for mediation and consensus-building.

However, certain aspects of the policy change remain unexplained. For instance, beginning in 1984 the administration repeatedly sought to reassure Moscow that Washington did not pose a threat to Soviet security. This came after three years of scoffing at the idea that Moscow could feel threatened by the West. In what way could Shultz and McFarlane have been responsible for such changes? Why would such reassurances be needed? This remains unclear. The administration's repeated references to "misunderstandings" and "miscalculations" between the superpowers also remain unexplained. And finally, this explanation does not clarify why there was such a sense of urgency surrounding the need for dialogue. Reagan had asserted that there was an "imperative" need for the two sides to talk. Abandoning the preconditions he had previously set before a summit could take place, the president had stated that he was "ready, willing and able" to "meet and talk anytime." It is not clear why, after eschewing summit meetings for three years, it would suddenly become imperative for the president to meet with his Soviet counterpart. Such a sense of urgency is certainly not in step with Shultz's calm, methodical approach to U.S.-Soviet relations.

George Shultz has repeatedly given President Reagan credit for initiating the more conciliatory approach to the Soviet Union. However, his assertions have largely been dismissed because people have clung tenaciously to the characterization of Reagan as a "no hands president." It has been assumed that the secretary was merely protecting a highly incompetent chief executive. Is it possible that Ronald Reagan caused U.S. policy to reverse course?

5

The Reagan Reversal
The Case for Leader-Driven Policy Change

> That dread makes its appearance is the pivot upon which
> everything turns. . . . He who is educated by dread is
> educated by possibility. . . . When such a person . . .
> knows that terror, perdition, and annihilation dwell next
> door to every man, and has learned the profitable lesson
> that every dread which alarms may the next instant
> become a fact, he will then interpret reality differently.
>
> *Soren Kierkegaard*[1]

THE PREVIOUS CHAPTER demonstrated that President Reagan was not always a "no hands president," allowing others to develop and execute his policies. Reagan did take control of U.S. foreign policy—but only in those issue areas that especially interested him. The president's feelings of vulnerability and his fear of nuclear annihilation led him to introduce the Strategic Defense Initiative. His concern for the safety of American citizens abroad led to the Iran-contra affair. This chapter considers whether similar concerns may have led the president to direct the reversal in U.S. Soviet policy. Drawing on cognitive psychology, it considers the possibility that Reagan reversed his confrontational course out of concern for the threat of an unwanted nuclear war with the Soviet Union. It begins with an examination of Ronald Reagan's fears regarding nuclear war and

---

1. Soren Kierkegaard, *The Concept of Dread* (1844; reprint, Princeton: Princeton University Press, 1957), 140, as quoted in James G. Blight, *The Shattered Crystal Ball: Fear and Learning in the Cuban Missile Crisis,* 3, xix.

his interpretation of the biblical story of Armageddon, then focuses on the events of the fall of 1983 and the effect they had on Reagan's perception of U.S.-Soviet relations.

Ronald Reagan had deeply held beliefs about the immorality of nuclear weapons and the strategic doctrines formed around them. "The concern about nuclear war and the challenge to diminish the threat of that war was always foremost in [Reagan's] mind," the president's longtime friend Martin Anderson once remarked. "It was not something he talked about a lot in public. But he had strong feelings and strong convictions about what could and should be done." Ed Meese, Reagan's former chief of staff in California and his counselor during his first presidential term, agrees. "What most puzzled Reagan's critics was his deep aversion to nuclear weapons and even the remotest prospect of nuclear war," Meese has noted. "[In this] he never wavered throughout his eight years at the White House." Secretary of State George Shultz concurs, asserting that the president deeply abhorred the superpowers' reliance on nuclear weapons. Shultz notes, however, that Reagan's feelings "were not remotely appreciated [by the public] or given much attention at the time."[2]

The president felt that the development of nuclear weapons represented a large step backward for mankind. "Looking back at the recent history of the world," he observed in his memoirs, "I find it amazing how civilization has retrogressed so quickly."

> As recently as World War I . . . we had a set of rules of warfare in which armies didn't make war against civilians: Soldiers fought soldiers. . . . By the time the 1980s rolled around, we were placing our entire faith in a weapon whose fundamental target was the civilian population. A nuclear war is aimed at people, no matter how often military men like to say, "No, we only aim to hit other missiles."[3]

2. Anderson, *Revolution,* 72; Edwin Meese III, *With Reagan: The Inside Story,* 186–87; Shultz, *Turmoil and Triumph,* 189.

3. Reagan, *An American Life,* 549. For similar sentiments, see Reagan, Interview with Representatives of NHK Television, Tokyo, Japan, November 11, 1983, *Public Papers 1983,* 1582.

Reagan was appalled by the destructive capacity of nuclear weapons, and he thought of this destruction in very human terms.

> One of the first statistics I saw as president was one of the most sober and startling I've ever heard. I'll never forget it: The Pentagon said at least 150 million American lives would be lost in a nuclear war with the Soviet Union—even if we "won." For Americans who survived such a war, I couldn't imagine what life would be like. The planet would be so poisoned the "survivors" would have no place to live. Even if nuclear war did not mean the extinction of mankind, it would certainly mean the end of civilization as we knew it. No one could "win" a nuclear war.[4]

"For the first time in history, man had the power to destroy mankind itself," Reagan wrote. "A war between the superpowers would incinerate much of the world and leave what was left of it uninhabitable forever."[5]

Reagan was also morally opposed to the doctrine of mutual assured destruction (MAD), which had been the foundation of arms control thinking for nearly forty years. As he described it, "MAD [was] madness. It was the craziest thing I ever heard of: Simply put, it called for each side to keep enough nuclear weapons at the ready to obliterate each other, so that if one attacked, the second had enough bombs left to annihilate its adversary in a matter of minutes. We were a button push away from oblivion. . . . ." Without defenses against nuclear missiles, both East and West would be deterred from launching a first strike by the fear of a retaliatory second strike against its own territory. The president likened this to "two westerners standing in a saloon aiming their guns at each other's head—permanently." Reagan longed to move away from what he saw as an extremely dangerous doctrine. "I've become more and more deeply convinced that the human spirit must be capable of rising above dealing with other nations and human beings by threatening their existence," he remarked in 1983. "[T]o

---

4. Reagan, *An American Life*, 550.
5. Ibid., 258. See also Reagan, Interview with NHK Television, November 11, 1983, *Public Papers 1983*, 1582.

rely on the specter of retaliation, on mutual threat . . . [is] a sad commentary on the human condition."[6]

Reagan remained opposed to the principle of mutual assured destruction despite the fact that many of his advisers believed it had been responsible for keeping the peace since World War II. "I told the president that I shared his dissatisfaction with our dependence on the threat of nuclear annihilation as the means of keeping the peace," Shultz has reflected. "But [I explained that] nuclear weapons cannot be uninvented." In late 1983 the secretary prepared a paper for Reagan outlining the reasons to stick with MAD. "But I made no real impact on the president with this line of reasoning," Shultz admits. "He stuck with his own deeply held view." Frank Carlucci, the president's fifth national security adviser, recalled similar experiences trying to win Reagan over to the virtues of MAD. "He would say to me that nuclear weapons are inherently evil. I'd respond with the traditional case for nuclear deterrence, saying that nuclear weapons had kept the peace for forty years." Reagan was never convinced. Likewise, Margaret Thatcher tried to persuade Reagan that MAD was essential, arguing that it had protected her country and Europe from the ravages of war since 1945. Again the president repudiated the idea. "I don't think there's any morality in that at all," he told her.[7]

The president was opposed to MAD for pragmatic reasons as well. He was deeply skeptical about the effectiveness of arms control treaties. Reagan's views on arms accords were profoundly shaped by a book by Laurence Beilenson entitled *The Treaty Trap: A History of the Performance of Political Treaties by the United States and European Nations*. Beilenson had been a lawyer for the Screen Actors Guild during Reagan's movie days, and the president considered the hardliner a good friend. The main premise of Beilenson's book is that nations only abide by treaties when it is in their interest to do so. All nations habitually renege on treaties once they feel no more use for them. Reagan called it "the best book written on defense" and asserted that it demonstrated that the Soviets would abrogate arms

6. Reagan, *An American Life*, 13, 547. Reagan, Address to the Nation, March 23, 1983, *WCPD* 19:447.

7. Shultz, *Turmoil and Triumph*, 466, 509; Cannon, *President Reagan*, 291.

treaties if they felt the accords threatened their interests. Indeed, the administration already had evidence that the Kremlin had exploited ambiguous language in existing treaties to its own advantage. The threat of nuclear war remained as long as the weapons themselves existed, Reagan believed. Existing arms control treaties did little to mitigate the threat of nuclear war that hung over the world. In a 1981 commencement speech at West Point Reagan remarked, "*The Treaty Trap* was the result of years of research, and it makes plain that no nation that placed its faith in parchment or paper, while at the same time it gave up on its protective hardware, ever lasted long enough to write many pages in history."[8]

Underpinning the president's abhorrence of nuclear weapons and MAD was his fascination with the biblical story of Armageddon. Reagan had grown up in a rather religious family. Although his father was Catholic, his mother was a member of the Disciples of Christ, and she raised Reagan in this tradition. Nelle Reagan figured prominently in shaping her son's religious views, emphasizing the role of religion in one's everyday life. Young Ronald Reagan was an active participant in his religious community, working at the church after school and taking part in a variety of youth programs, including periodic plays that constituted his first experience with acting. He even dated the pastor's daughter for eight years. As Garry Wills puts it, Reagan "was as close to being a 'minister's kid' as one can be without actually moving into the rectory." Reagan later chose to attend a college run by the Disciples of Christ, and socialized primarily with other members of the church during his early adult years.[9]

Like his mother, Ronald Reagan had an intimate knowledge of the bible and, in accord with the Disciples' traditions, he interpreted the bible literally. Consequently, the president interpreted the story of Armageddon as a prophecy of the end of the earth by nuclear

---

8. Reagan, Address at the Commencement Exercises at the United States Military Academy, May 27, 1981, *WCPD* 17:564; R. Scheer, "Nuclear War a Real Prospect to Reagan Hard-Liners," *Chicago Sun-Times,* October 4, 1981, 1. For more on the influence of *The Treaty Trap* on Reagan, see Anderson, *Revolution,* 74–75; and Glad, "Black-and-White Thinking."

9. Gary Wills, *Reagan's America: Innocents at Home,* 17–18.

war. "The president had fairly strong views about the parable of Armageddon," National Security Adviser Robert McFarlane has confided. "He believed that a nuclear exchange would be the fulfillment of that prophecy [and that] the world would end through a nuclear catastrophe." Such views were strengthened by Reagan's contacts with the Reverend Billy Graham, whom Reagan first met in the late 1960s. As Reagan interpreted the parable, an acclaimed leader from the West would defeat the Soviets in a great battle. After achieving victory, the Western leader would then be revealed as the Antichrist. He too would fall, and Jesus Christ would triumph in the creation of a new Heaven and Earth. In the biblical story there is a plague that destroys a large army from the Orient. Reagan maintained that this plague was to be a nuclear war, citing its description of "the eyes burning from the head and the hair falling from the body and so forth."[10]

Reagan also believed that world conditions during the 1970s and 1980s were right for Armageddon to occur. Some of the important portents, he maintained, were the founding of the state of Israel, the fact that Libya had become communist, abnormal weather patterns, and natural disasters. In 1971 he told a prominent member of the California senate that the end of the world was near because, for the first time, events were falling into place according to the biblical prophecy. "We may be the generation that sees Armageddon," Reagan confided nine years later in an interview on Jim Bakker's PTL television network. During the mid-1980s the president repeated this view privately to a number of political and business figures, much to the dismay of his political advisers who tried to steer him away from such talk. In a February 1985 interview with *The Wall Street Journal* Reagan again brought up the subject of Armageddon with the reporters. "I don't know whether you know, but a great many theologians over a number of years . . . have been struck with the fact that in recent years, as in no other time in history, most of the prophecies have been coming together."[11]

10. McFarlane interview, July 7, 1995; Cannon, *President Reagan*, 288–90. See also Reagan, *My Early Life*; and Reagan, *An American Life*, part 1.

11. Cannon, *President Reagan*, 289–90; Reagan, Interview with *People Magazine*, December 6, 1983, *Public Papers 1983*, 1714–15; Mayer and McManus, *Landslide*,

Reagan most feared that a nuclear accident, or a renegade with nuclear armaments, would precipitate nuclear Armageddon. "We all know how to make [nuclear] missiles," Reagan remarked. "One day a madman could come along and make the missiles and blackmail all of us—but not if we have a defense against them." The president hoped the Strategic Defense Initiative would prevent against such scenarios. "The president had a spiritual foreboding about nuclear Armageddon," McFarlane has explained, and believed it was his responsibility to try to protect Americans via SDI. In March 1983 Reagan asked Americans, "[What if] we could intercept and destroy strategic ballistic missiles before they reached our own soil or that of our allies? . . . Wouldn't it be better to save lives than to avenge them?"[12]

Reagan believed that the presence of vast quantities of nuclear weapons raised the probability of a nuclear accident. The very existence of these weapons, he asserted, threatened people around the globe. Therefore, the president rejected traditional approaches to arms control. Previous arms accords, such as SALT I and SALT II, had focused on limiting the growth of nuclear arsenals. Reagan wanted to *reduce* those arsenals. His ultimate goal was the elimination of nuclear weapons. "As long as nuclear weapons were in existence," he asserted, "there would always be risks they would be used, and once the first weapon was unleashed, who knew where it would end? My dream then, became a world free of nuclear weapons."[13]

Reagan's ideas on arms control were quite unconventional at the time. As Martin Anderson has noted,

---

33–34. Reagan's views about Armageddon also came up during the 1984 election campaign, during the president's second debate with Walter Mondale. See Kenneth L. Woodward, "Arguing Armageddon," *Newsweek* (November 5, 1984), 91.

12. Reagan, *An American Life,* 548, 550; McFarlane interview, July 7, 1995; Reagan, Address to the Nation, March 23, 1983, WCPD 19:447–48. Of course, it can be argued that Reagan's advocacy of SDI and the elimination of nuclear weapons was illogical given his literal interpretation of the Armageddon story. If the parable was indeed foretelling the end of the world, it would make little sense to try to stop something that was preordained.

13. Reagan, *An American Life,* 550.

> The conventional wisdom on nuclear weapons was very clear
> during the late 1970s. . . . Virtually no one at the time thought
> seriously that there was a chance of any reduction in nuclear
> missiles. In fact, during the late 1970s and the early 1980s, the
> most radical proposal put forth was a freeze on existing nuclear
> stockpiles. . . . And when Reagan began to talk privately of a
> dream he had when someday we might live in a world free of
> all nuclear missiles, well, we just smiled.[14]

Although Reagan had strong views about the immorality of nuclear
weapons and deep fears regarding the prospect of nuclear catastrophe,
these views remained largely hidden from the public. Such beliefs
would be difficult to articulate to the American public, Reagan's
advisers maintained, especially given the media's appetite for juicy
sound bites. Aides feared that the president's remarks would be misinterpreted and used against him. They also felt that such sentiments
could jeopardize the administration's military buildup, a program they
did not intend to abandon.[15]

Keeping Reagan's strong feelings about nuclear war in mind, con-
cepts from cognitive psychology can be used to explain how a series
of events in the fall of 1983 may have led the president to believe that
a change in U.S. Soviet policy was imperative. Three events in the
fall of 1983—the downing of KAL Flight 007, the television movie
"The Day After," and a Pentagon briefing on nuclear war—could have
made the issue of nuclear annihilation especially salient for Reagan
in late 1983. The prospect of nuclear war was "on his mind," so to
speak. Available evidence indicates that shortly after these incidents
Reagan had a turning-point experience. In early November, NATO
conducted a military exercise in Europe called "Able Archer." Moscow
misperceived this drill to be the initial stages of a nuclear first strike
against them, and, in response, prepared its own nuclear forces for
a retaliatory attack. Though there was no actual nuclear exchange,
Reagan viewed the incident as a nuclear "near-miss." Exercise Able

14. Anderson, *Revolution,* 73.
15. Weinberger interview, July 31, 1995; and McFarlane interview, July 7, 1995.

Archer had brought the world to the brink of an inadvertent nuclear war, he believed. This horrific realization led the president to take charge of U.S. Soviet policy and to shift to a more conciliatory approach to Moscow.

Before examining these events in detail, it is important to understand what cognitive psychologists call "priming effects." Priming "describes the effects of prior context on the interpretation of new information. . . . It refers to the fact that recently and frequently activated ideas come to mind more easily than ideas that have not been activated."[16] Simply put, prior experiences can lead to certain ideas being "on one's mind." These ideas can then influence one's interpretation of subsequent events. If, for example, one is repeatedly reminded about sexism, perhaps through reading about it, or discussing it with friends, then one is more likely to perceive sexism in daily life.

Individuals habitually assimilate new information to categories or ideas—called the "prime"—that have been primed. Moreover, the more ambiguous the new information, the more likely it is to be assimilated to the prime. For instance, in their study on priming effects, Higgins, Rholes, and Jones divided subjects into two groups. One group was subjected to negative priming. That is, they were exposed to a series of subliminal phrases describing negative traits, such as "reckless." The other group was exposed to a series of positive traits, such as "adventurous." Both groups were then shown pictures of people shooting rapids in a canoe, and asked to assess the scenario. The subjects that had been exposed to negative phrases were far more likely to offer negative evaluations. To these subjects, the people shooting the rapids were acting irresponsibly, and needlessly endangering themselves. Subjects who had been exposed to positive terms, however, were more likely to have a positive assessment of the behavior.[17]

16. Susan T. Fiske and Shelley E. Taylor, *Social Cognition,* 257.
17. E. T. Higgins, W. S. Rholes, and C. R. Jones, "Category Accessibility and Impression Formation." See also P. M. Herr, S. J. Sherman, and R. H. Fazio, "On the Consequences of Priming: Assimilation and Contrast Effects."

Additional studies show that priming effects are both prevalent and powerful. Priming can lead people to significantly alter their opinions on a wide range of topics. Even strongly held views can be changed as a result of priming. "It is striking," write psychologists Susan Fiske and Shelley Taylor, "that all kinds of responses, from temporary states to initial judgements, to seemingly well-established opinions, all change with priming." Priming can also cause people to revise their assessments of national policies. For example, Roger Tourangeau and colleagues found that priming affected subjects' attitudes toward aid to the Nicaraguan contras and support for SDI.[18]

Priming can change one's emotional state as well as one's judgements. For instance, Roxana Robles and colleagues found that self-reported levels of anxiety were significantly increased for subjects who had been subliminally primed with threatening images. Priming can even alter one's behavior. Other research has demonstrated that subjects primed for hostility behave in a more antagonistic, competitive way than do subjects who have not been primed.[19]

"Availability effects" are associated with priming effects. Introduced by Amos Tversky and Daniel Kahneman in 1973, this concept refers to the fact that certain scenarios may be remembered more easily than others. They are more readily "available" in one's mind. The ease with which one remembers a specific scenario affects one's judgement of how likely that event is to occur. For example, most people can easily recall an image of a plane crash, as these disasters are routinely covered by television news programs. Because air disasters are "mentally available," we overestimate their likelihood. We assume that plane crashes are more likely to occur than they actually are. In an experiment testing the availability effect and its relationship to judgements of probability, Tversky and Kahneman asked subjects which was more prevalent in English, words that began with the letter "k," or words in which "k" appeared as the third letter. Words beginning with the letter "k" are much easier to recall. Therefore, the vast majority of

18. Fiske and Taylor, *Social Cognition,* 257–65.
19. Roxana Robles, R. Smith, C. Carver, and A. R. Wellens, "Influence of Subliminal Visual Images on the Experience of Anxiety"; P. M. Herr, "Consequences of Priming: Judgement and Behavior."

subjects replied that words beginning with "k" were more prevalent. In fact, there are more words in which "k" is the third letter. Tversky and Kahneman concluded that mental availability affects judgments of probability. That is, events are judged more likely to occur if they come readily to mind. People have the "tendency to predict the outcome that is most easily remembered or imagined."[20]

Availability effects also come into play when one is asked to predict future events. Imagining hypothetical future events makes those events seem more probable. For instance, in the early 1970s John S. Carroll found that subjects asked to mentally rehearse a hypothetical scenario in which Gerald Ford won the 1976 presidential election later rated it more probable that Ford would actually win, as compared with a group that did not mentally rehearse such a scenario. Scenarios that are mentally rehearsed, this study found, are judged more likely to occur.[21]

During the fall of 1983, President Reagan had been primed to think about nuclear war; three different events forced Reagan to contemplate the realities of nuclear Armageddon. This priming had two effects. First, it led him to conclude that the likelihood of nuclear war was greater than he had thought earlier. The scenario of nuclear war was mentally "available," and therefore, judged more probable. And second, priming affected the way the president interpreted subsequent events that fall, particularly the events surrounding Able Archer.

KAL 007

On September 1, 1983, a Soviet SU-15 jet fighter shot down a Korean airliner flying from Alaska to Seoul. All 269 people on board were killed, including 61 Americans.

20. Amos Tversky and Daniel Kahneman, "Availability: A Heuristic for Judging Frequency and Probability"; George, *Presidential Decisionmaking*, 60.

21. The same effect was found for a group that mentally rehearsed a victory for Carter. John S. Carroll, "The Effect of Imagining an Event on Expectations of the Event: An Interpretation in Terms of the Availability Heuristic." See also Robert P. Abelson and Ariel Levi, "Decision Making and Decision Theory," 282.

The Reagan administration publicly condemned the incident as "an act of barbarism." Privately, however, Reagan officials were receiving increasing evidence that the incident had been caused by a series of human errors. There were indications that the crew had set the plane's automatic pilot system incorrectly, allowing it to stray more than three hundred miles into Soviet airspace. The pilots flying KAL 007 never gave any indication that they were aware they were off course in their communications with international ground control stations. Such a mechanical error was not unknown. In fact, there had been over one hundred instances of airliners straying significantly from their intended flight path because of navigation errors.[22]

More tragically, the Soviets mistook the civilian plane to be a U.S. military aircraft. Earlier that evening a U.S. intelligence plane had briefly crossed KAL 007's flight path as it neared Soviet airspace. Most likely, Soviet military analysts assumed the Korean aircraft was the U.S. reconnaissance plane.

Subsequent Soviet efforts to identify and intercept the plane were chaotic. KAL Flight 007 had gone nearly three hundred miles into Soviet airspace and was approaching one of the USSR's most militarily sensitive regions near Vladivostok before a Soviet defense aircraft was able to get near it. Although the SU-15 fired warning shots at the South Korean plane, the crew most likely did not see them, as the shots were fired from below the aircraft just as it was climbing to a higher altitude. With its nose pointed upward, the Korean pilot would not have been able to see the flares below. The Soviets also violated their own rules of engagement by not visually identifying the plane before launching an attack. The Soviet pilot, Lieutenant Colonel Gennadi Osipovich, noted KAL's flashing navigation lights, but was unable to give a fuller description of the aircraft. After much scrambling and making nervous calls to Moscow, Soviet ground officials anxiously reminded the pilot

22. Reagan, "U.S. Measures in Response to the Soviets' Korean Airline Massacre," September 5, 1983, *AFP:CD 1983*, 545–46; Richard Witkin, "Downing of KAL 007 Laid to Russian Error," *New York Times*, June 16, 1993. For detailed accounts of the KAL 007 incident, see Seymour M. Hersh, *The Target is Destroyed*; Alexander Dallin, *Black Box*; and R. W. Johnson, *Shootdown: The Verdict on KAL 007*.

that visual identification was imperative. Osipovich failed to do this, however, presumably because he felt his target's running lights told him enough.

These mistakes were compounded by the failure of U.S. intelligence agencies to adequately monitor the situation. U.S. Air Force communications intelligence units in Alaska and northern Japan intercepted Soviet transmissions for over two and a half hours, listening as the Soviets began tracking and pursuing the ill-fated flight. Western intelligence officials erroneously assumed the Soviets were conducting a routine exercise, albeit at an odd time of the night. Moreover, U.S. intelligence analysts in the area listened to the downing as it happened, failing to comprehend for hours what had actually taken place.

The president and his advisers were deeply disturbed that the Soviets could have made such an error. The Russians had tracked the plane for over two hours before shooting it down. There had been plenty of time for Moscow to institute crisis procedures and to notify Washington of the intrusion. But there had been no communication between the two capitals. "If they thought this was a commercial airliner, there is no excuse," Shultz told his colleagues at the time. "But if they thought it was a U.S. intelligence plane and tracked it and didn't contact us, that is also an extremely serious matter." When the CIA and the National Security Agency later informed the secretary that they believed the Soviets had mistaken the identity of the aircraft, Shultz responded, "this is still terribly disturbing." Two hundred sixty-nine lives had been lost because of a series of miscalculations and a breakdown in communication between Washington and Moscow. Human errors had caused a tragedy. This point was not lost on Reagan, who was especially disturbed by the larger implications of the KAL disaster. Interestingly, he linked the tragedy to his fears about an accidental nuclear war. "If anything," he reflected, "the KAL incident demonstrated how close the world had come to the precipice and how much we needed nuclear arms control. If . . . the Soviet pilots simply mistook the airliner for a military plane, what kind of imagination did it take to think of a Soviet military man with his finger close to a nuclear button making an even more tragic mistake? If mistakes could be made by a fighter pilot, what about a similar miscalculation by the commander of missile launch crew?"[23]

"The Day After"

Five weeks later the president was again forced to confront his fears about nuclear war. On October 10, 1983, Reagan privately screened the television movie "The Day After," which ABC planned to air on November 20. As *The Washington Post* described it, the film was a "horrific vision of nuclear holocaust."[24] "The Day After" depicted the destruction of Lawrence, Kansas, and surrounding areas following a nuclear exchange between the United States and the Soviet Union. The subject of nuclear war had been dealt with before on film, but never in such a graphic and hard-hitting manner. Previously, the issue was usually examined from a scientific perspective and in a documentary format. "The Day After" took a different approach. It was anecdotal, focusing on the daily lives of the people in Lawrence. The audience gained a certain amount of familiarity with the townspeople and what life was like in their small midwestern city. This sense of familiarity made the subsequent events all the more horrific. "The Day After" followed these people as the nuclear catastrophe was occurring, powerfully relating the town's destruction. The film was unusually graphic, detailing the burns, radiation sickness, and famine that Americans would likely suffer as a result of such an event.

The movie received much media attention before it aired. For several days before the broadcast, newspapers ran articles warning of the movie's graphic nature and suggesting that individuals not watch the movie alone. Naturally, part of this media hype was due to ABC's efforts to boost its ratings. But there was genuine concern about the impact the movie might have on those watching it. Churches, social groups, and civic organizations formed support groups for people to watch

23. Shultz, *Turmoil and Triumph,* 362–63; Reagan, *An American Life,* 584.
24. Reagan, *An American Life,* 585. See also Peter Perl, " 'The Day After': Nation Girds for Firestorm," *Washington Post,* November 20, 1983.

the movie together and then to discuss it afterward. Special phone lines were set up to provide counseling for those having difficulties with what they saw. There was special concern over the impact the movie might have on children. Calling the movie "powerful, gripping, graphic, and depressing," the National Association of Independent Schools sent a letter to parents and faculty nationwide suggesting ways for adults to approach the topic with children. The National Education Association sent out its first-ever national alert about the movie, suggesting, among other things, that children under 12 not be allowed to view the film. The New York City School Board sent out the following memo:

> ABC's intention in presenting ["The Day After"] is to educate the public about nuclear war. However, the scenes of terrible destruction, people being vaporized, mass graves, and death from radiation sickness may NOT be helpful or educational for children or young people. This is not just one more horror film. Adults can confidently tell youngsters that ghosts and vampires do not exist. But the threat of nuclear war is real.[25]

It is easy to skip lightly over this incident, dismissing its impact on any subsequent changes in policy. With most presidents this would probably be worthy of a footnote, at best. But there is reason to pause and examine the movie and the president's reaction to it more closely. First, it is important to understand that Ronald Reagan is an anecdotal thinker. He expresses his views through stories, most of them revolving around ordinary human beings. Anecdotes are Reagan's preferred style of communication when trying to make a point. Critics and supporters alike have remarked on the president's vast stockpile of stories and his gifts as a storyteller. Reagan "started nearly every meeting with a story," observed Donald Regan, treasury secretary and chief of staff in the Reagan administration. "The president knew more stories than anyone I had ever met." According to economist Alan Greenspan, his boss "used anecdotes to express his fundamental ideas and his attitude toward life." This was illustrated

25. Perl, " 'The Day After,' " *Washington Post*, November 20, 1983.

in the president's turning-point address in January 1984, in which the administration began to emphasize its common interests with the Soviet Union. Reagan wanted to argue that beneath all the politics and the ideological differences, Soviets and Americans are simply human beings, united in their concern for their children's welfare and the stability of their daily lives. Rather than convey his beliefs in an analytical fashion, Reagan spun the tale of Jim and Sally and their accidental meeting with Ivan and Anya as they all sought shelter in a driving rainstorm.[26]

More importantly for the present purposes, Reagan retained information more readily if it was relayed to him in a narrative style. He was not an analytical thinker. "Reagan shunned the abstract, the theoretical, the cold and impersonal approach to problems," wrote Don Regan. "His love of stories was connected to his tendency to see everything in human terms." After extensive interviews with members of the Reagan administration, Leslie Gelb concluded that "parables . . . seem to be central to the way the president's mind works. Often, it is not the logic of an argument that he remembers . . . but a circumstance or story that connects the issue at hand to his basic principles. And these anecdotes, his staff says, are often the last word on the matter. . . ." As Richard M. Pious bluntly put it, "Reagan could only understand things if they were presented in a story; he could only explain something if he narrated it; he could only think about principles if they involved metaphor and analogy."[27]

Reagan's aides were aware of this presidential trait and knew they had a better chance of getting their points across if they catered to his anecdotal style. In order to grab Reagan's attention at their morning meetings, Chief of Staff Regan used to preface his comments with a story or joke.[28] National Security Adviser William Clark, who had been with Reagan since the 1960s, used to coach people in the White

26. Reagan wrote the "Ivan and Anya" section of his turning-point address himself. Matlock interview, September 19, 1995. See also Cannon, *President Reagan*, 120–42; Leslie Gelb, "The Mind of the President"; and Regan, *For the Record*, 278.

27. Regan, *For the Record*, 278; Gelb, "The Mind of the President," 32; Richard M. Pious, "Prerogative Power and the Reagan Presidency," 500.

28. Regan, *For the Record*.

House, "If you think there are particular points you want to score [with the president], you're going to have to dress them up a bit, tie them to a metaphor [or] an analogy, and put a little sex appeal in it." Lou Cannon observed that

> all the lawyers who knew Reagan well—Clark, Meese, Darman, Weinberger, William French Smith—realized that Reagan took a different intellectual approach than they did. All of these lawyers also recognized that they could reach Reagan if they were willing to tune into his mental wavelength. The problem was that Reagan's reliance on metaphor and analogy for understanding made him vulnerable to arguments that were short on facts and long on theatrical gimmicks.[29]

In order to cater to the president's preference for anecdotes, Reagan's foreign policy advisers began briefing him through films rather than through the traditional briefing books replete with figures and jargon. Aware of Reagan's general lack of interest in foreign affairs, National Security Adviser Clark sought to capture the president's attention by showing him Defense Department videotapes on international politics. Using the White House theater, Clark showed the president movies on the Middle East and arms control. The Central Intelligence Agency began to utilize the same method in its presidential briefings. In order to prepare Reagan for an international visit, the CIA would develop short videos—often lasting only eight minutes or so—on the countries and leaders he would encounter. "The Agency started producing some great stuff that was enjoyable for all of us," Clark commented. "It was far more interesting to see a movie on Indira Gandhi, covering her life, than sitting down with the usual tome the Agency would produce. And that would spark questions from the president that I could fire back to the Agency. I knew from Sacramento days that he liked celluloid. After all, it was his profession."[30]

"The Day After," therefore, was especially well suited to Reagan's intellect. The film's format and style were perfect for impressing upon

29. Cannon, *President Reagan*, 151–52.
30. Cannon, *President Reagan*, 156–57; author interviews with anonymous officials. See also Woodward, *Veil*, 248–49.

the president the reality and horrors of nuclear war. It spoke to his fears about a nuclear Armageddon; it was narrative in style; and, like most of Reagan's own stories, it focused on the lives of ordinary Americans. The movie also presented the concept of nuclear annihilation in visual images that would stay with Reagan far longer than jargon-laden statistics.

Moreover, it is important to keep in mind that psychological studies have found that movies can cause people to think more about specific issues. Films can make certain topics more salient. For example, Shanto Iyengar and colleagues found that television news programs greatly influenced peoples' perceptions of which issues were most important for the president to address. The more news programs covered a specific issue, the more salient the issue became for people, and the more they felt the president needed to address the issue.[31]

Similar studies have concluded that "The Day After" had a significant impact on people's thoughts about nuclear war. Stanley Feldman and Lee Sigelman conducted a study in which they compared individuals' views on nuclear war before and after they viewed the television movie. Feldman and Sigelman found that the issue of nuclear war became especially salient for people after watching the film. This effect lasted for weeks. "[W]atching 'The Day After,' " they concluded, "had a significant impact on the reported salience of nuclear war, with viewers giving higher estimates of the amount of time they spent thinking about nuclear war [after they had seen the movie than before they had viewed it]." Viewing "The Day After" led subjects to consider the possibility of nuclear war far more frequently than they had prior to seeing the movie. Consequently, they sought out more information on the issue, reading more about the topic in the print media. More importantly for the present purposes, Feldman and Sigelman found that "the more news stories about nuclear war one watched or read,

31. For example, see Stephen J. Fitzsimmons and Hobart G. Osburn, "The Impact of Social Issues and Public Affairs Television Documentaries"; and Lee Sigelman and Carol K. Sigelman, "The Politics of Popular Culture: Campaign Cynicism and 'The Candidate.'" Shanto Iyengar, Mark D. Peters, Donald R. Kinder, "Experimental Demonstrations of the 'Not-So-Minimal' Consequences of Television News Programs."

the more likely one was to move toward a more conciliatory approach to U.S.-Soviet relations. This is a powerful effect."[32]

Feldman and Sigelman's research focused on mass opinions and therefore cannot be used to predict an individual's views. However, the president himself has indicated that "The Day After" made a lasting impression on him. Seven years after seeing the film, Reagan wrote about the impact the movie had on him in his memoirs. "Other events that autumn besides the KAL incident made me aware of the need for the world to step back from the nuclear precipice," he recollects. "This was part of the entry in my diary for October 10, 1983:"

> In the morning at Camp David I ran the tape of the movie ABC is running on Nov. 20. It's called "The Day After" in which Lawrence, Kansas, is wiped out in a nuclear war with Russia. It is powerfully done, all $7 million worth. It is very effective and left me greatly depressed. So far they haven't sold any of the 25 ads scheduled and I can see why. . . . My own reaction: we have to do all we can . . . to see that there is never a nuclear war.[33]

Pentagon Briefing on Nuclear War

Shortly after previewing "The Day After" Reagan had to contemplate the realities of nuclear Armageddon yet again. Toward the end of October 1983 the president participated in a Pentagon briefing on U.S. nuclear war plans, the Single Integrated Operational Plan (SIOP). Led by Defense Secretary Weinberger and Chairman of the Joint Chiefs of Staff John Vessey, the meeting took place in the Situation Room.

During the briefing Weinberger and Vessey explained to the president that the U.S. nuclear arsenal was targeting over fifty thousand sites in the Soviet Union. Only half of these targets were military sites. The rest consisted of economic and industrial locations, as well as concentrations of human beings. The United States was now targeting the Soviet leadership to a greater extent than it had in the past, in the belief that this increased threat would make the Kremlin less inclined

---

32. Stanley Feldman and Lee Sigelman, "The Political Impact of Prime-Time Television: 'The Day After.'"

33. Reagan, *An American Life*, 585.

to launch a nuclear first strike. The officials also explained that if the United States were to carry out this plan, Soviet nuclear retaliation was almost certain. Such retaliatory strikes, they cautioned, would destroy Washington, if not the entire country.

Although the Pentagon had routinely briefed U.S. presidents on U.S. nuclear war plans, Reagan had resisted attending such meetings for the first two years he was in office. The president had been disturbed at the thought of rehearsing nuclear Armageddon, and much to his officials' dismay, he had refused to take part. Indeed, Reagan was nearly the first modern president not to receive the SIOP briefing. In 1983 Pentagon officials twisted the president's arm, persuading him that his presence was a necessity. Reluctantly, he consented.

According to those present, Reagan was "chastened" by what he witnessed and became withdrawn. Weinberger has attested that the president found the briefing to be a terribly disturbing experience. "He had a very deep revulsion to the whole idea of nuclear weapons," the defense secretary explained. "These war games brought home to anybody the fantastically horrible events that would surround such a scenario." Afterwards, Reagan called the meeting "a most sobering experience," and likened it to "The Day After." "In several ways, the sequence of events described in the briefings paralleled those in the ABC movie," he remarked. "Simply put, it was a scenario for a sequence of events that could lead to the end of civilization as we knew it. . . ." With scenes of nuclear annihilation still fresh in his mind from "The Day After," Reagan was distressed by his knowledge of Washington's preparations for such an event. Reagan, who abhorred the reliance on nuclear weapons, felt these plans ignored the human factor in nuclear strategy. "There are still some people at the Pentagon who claim a nuclear war is 'winnable,' " the president complained after the briefing. "I thought they were crazy." A few weeks after Reagan took part in this meeting he ordered his aides and scientists to "speed up" research on the Strategic Defense Initiative. "I was convinced we had to do everything possible to develop a defense against those horrible weapons of mass destruction," he added.[34]

---

34. Reagan, *An American Life,* 585; interviews with anonymous officials; Oberdorfer, *The Turn,* 56; Desmond Ball and Robert C. Toth, "Revising the SIOP: Taking

In sum, during the fall of 1983 the president was primed to think about nuclear war. Within a short time period Reagan was repeatedly forced to confront his fears about nuclear annihilation. The KAL 007 disaster caused Reagan to contemplate the possibility of a miscalculation involving nuclear weapons. "The Day After" presented him with visual images of nuclear annihilation and left him "greatly depressed." Reagan's own comments, and Feldman and Sigelman's study, suggest that the movie made the issue of nuclear war highly salient for the president. The subsequent Pentagon briefing compelled Reagan to contemplate the realities of nuclear war yet again.

As noted earlier, priming affects the way in which individuals interpret new information. People tend to assimilate new information to the prime, especially if the information is ambiguous. This suggests that if Reagan was primed to think about nuclear war, he would assimilate new information to this prime. He would be more likely to perceive new experiences through the "lens" of nuclear war.

Moreover, given the availability effect, Reagan would perceive the probability of nuclear war occurring as greater than it objectively was. As Robert Abelson and Ariel Levi note, "[I]n the case of hypothetical future outcomes, in which past data are scarce, availability may devolve on the [mental] rehearsal of relevant event scenarios that have been provided. . . ."[35] In other words, Reagan "mentally rehearsed" the scenario of a nuclear war through viewing "The Day After" and by participating in the Pentagon briefing. Consequently, he also increased the mental availability of that scenario. According to the availability heuristic, the more easily one can recall a scenario, the more one believes that scenario is likely to occur.

Able Archer 83

During November 2–11, 1983, the United States and its NATO allies conducted a large-scale military exercise called "Able Archer 83." The

---

War-Fighting to Dangerous Extremes"; Richard Halloran, "Reagan as Commander in Chief," 57.

35. Abelson and Levi, "Decision Making and Decision Theory," 282.

purpose of this exercise was to practice nuclear release mechanisms. NATO forces simulated the command and communications procedures that would be employed during a nuclear strike against the Eastern bloc.[36]

Although NATO had conducted similar exercises in the past, Able Archer 83 was far more extensive than any of NATO's previous war games. Extending from Scandinavia to the Mediterranean, the drill employed more than three hundred thousand military and civilian personnel according to some estimates. Able Archer 83 was also more realistic than its predecessors. Although "principals"—heads of state, defense ministers, and the like—had never participated in such drills before, the original plans for the 1983 exercise called for these officials to take part. In the United States, the president, vice president, defense secretary, and Joint Chiefs of Staff were slated to participate in the simulated nuclear attack. Reagan officials ultimately scaled back these plans, however. "I had serious misgivings about approving the drill as originally planned," Robert McFarlane has confided. "There were concerns that superpower relations were too tense. There was a concern with how Moscow would perceive such a realistic drill." Because of the high state of anxiety between East and West, it was finally decided that President Reagan would not take part in the exercise, but that other leaders would participate in a staggered sequence. British Prime Minister Margaret Thatcher and German Chancellor Helmut Kohl played integral roles in the drill, although they did not participate simultaneously.[37]

As was usual, the Soviet Union and its Warsaw Pact allies monitored Able Archer through electronic listening devices in Eastern Europe. As they eavesdropped, the Soviets became alarmed by what they

36. Information on Able Archer comes from interviews with McFarlane, Weinberger, Matlock, and other, anonymous, sources. See also Christopher Andrew and Oleg Gordievsky, *KGB: The Inside Story,* 502–7; Gordon Brook-Shepherd, *The Storm Birds,* xii, 266–71; Murrey Marder, "Defector Told of Soviet Alert," *Washington Post,* August 8, 1986; and transcript from "Ideas" (radio program on Operation RYAN), Canadian Broadcasting Corporation [CBC], November 4–5, 1992.

37. Interviews with McFarlane and anonymous officials; "Ustinov: USSR Will Counter Euromissiles," *CDSP,* 35:46, 6–7.

detected. Historically, Soviet leaders had long been concerned about the possibility of a "madman" ascending to the U.S. presidency. "This was one of the ways that [the Soviets] thought a nuclear war might really happen," Soviet expert Franklyn Griffiths has explained, "that is, if an 'adventurer,' as they put it, came to the White House."[38] Since 1981 the Kremlin had been growing increasingly fearful that Ronald Reagan was just such an adventurer, and that a nuclear attack against the Soviet Union was imminent. Moscow had expected Reagan, once in office, to tone down his anti-Soviet rhetoric and to endorse detente, much as Richard Nixon had done. Instead, Reagan had employed increasingly threatening rhetoric and initiated a large-scale military buildup. Since the Soviets believed there was relative military parity between the two superpowers, they felt that the U.S. buildup was an attempt to gain military superiority over the USSR. The Soviets felt especially threatened by the Strategic Defense Initiative. SDI, they maintained, would broaden the scope of the arms race. It was also destabilizing. Previously, the Americans had been deterred from launching a nuclear first strike against the East because they feared a retaliatory strike from Moscow. If the proposed shield was successful in protecting the U.S. from nuclear attack, the Americans would no longer be deterred from launching a nuclear first strike.[39]

The Kremlin also detected important and threatening changes in the United States' war-fighting strategy. Reagan administration officials had implied that the United States was more willing to utilize its nuclear armaments than previous administrations had been. In October 1981 the president suggested that the United States could participate in a limited nuclear war. Reagan told reporters that he could envision a situation in which tactical nuclear weapons could be employed "against troops in the field without it bringing either one of the major powers to pushing the button." Several weeks later Secretary of State Haig spoke about the possibility of firing what he called "a nuclear warning shot." Moreover, Moscow felt especially threatened by the Reagan administration's nuclear

38. "Ideas," CBC, 4.

39. Seweryn Bialer and Joan Afferica, "Reagan and Russia," 250–53; Jerry F. Hough, "The World as Viewed from Moscow."

war-fighting plans, which placed greater emphasis on targeting the Soviet leadership.[40]

The Reagan White House had also rebuffed Soviet calls for a "no first use" agreement. Moscow wanted Washington to agree that neither side would introduce nuclear weapons into a conventional conflict. The president said that he didn't think "any useful purpose is served in making such a declaration." "Unfortunately," he continued, "our strategic nuclear weapons are the only balance or deterrent that we have to the massive buildup of conventional arms that the Soviet Union has on the NATO front." In order to deter the Eastern bloc from initiating a conventional attack against Western Europe, the United States had to reserve the right to respond with nuclear weapons. This was not a change in the American position; the United States had never had a "no first use" policy. However, within the context of the Reagan administration's rhetoric and its large military buildup, this rebuff caused concern in Moscow. The Kremlin perceived the American position to be offensive in nature, not defensive. Moscow knew that it was not planning to attack Western Europe, and assumed the West understood this. Therefore, the American refusal to commit to a "no first use" agreement was perceived to be the equivalent of advocating a nuclear first-strike policy.[41]

Compounding this, the Reagan administration had established an image of military unpredictability. Displays of military force had been an integral part of U.S. foreign policy. In the sixteen months before Able Archer, Reagan had dispatched marines and warships to Lebanon, sent military forces to Central America, and mounted a military show of force against Libya. And on October 25, 1983, only one week before Able Archer began, the United States had invaded Grenada—for the purpose of ousting communist "thugs." "Collectively, [these incidents] helped create the impression of a president prepared to use force in support of American interests," commented political scientist Michael Mandelbaum in 1985. "Although it cannot

40. Reagan, News Conference, November 10, 1981, *WCPD* 17:1243–44; Ball and Toth, "Revising the SIOP," 69, 74.
41. Reagan, News Conference, May 13, 1982, *WCPD* 18:636; Ralph K. White, "Empathizing with the Rulers of the USSR," 121–26.

be proven, it is not unreasonable to suppose that this impression has entered the calculations of others from time to time over the last five years, to the advantage of the United States."[42] It is also not unreasonable to suppose that this impression entered into others' calculations to the potential detriment of the United States.

Finally, the KAL 007 incident contributed to Soviet fears about a nuclear attack by the West. Many within the Soviet leadership, including General Secretary Andropov and the chief of staff of the armed forces, Marshal Nikolai Ogarkov, maintained that the South Korean aircraft had been on an American intelligence mission. KAL 007, they asserted, had been photographing Soviet defenses, or at minimum, testing Soviet radar. Even those who doubted that KAL 007 was involved in espionage still believed that the Reagan administration had blown the incident out of proportion and was using it to whip up anti-Soviet hysteria internationally. The American reaction to the KAL incident added to the already-present fears about U.S. intentions.[43]

The KAL 007 tragedy also made Moscow acutely aware of its own vulnerability. The 747 had been in Soviet airspace for over two hours before Soviet air defense forces were able to approach the aircraft. Even more disturbing, eight of the eleven Soviet tracking stations on the Kamchatka Peninsula and Sakhalin Island had failed to detect the plane. Subsequent communications within the Soviet military were characterized by chaos. For the Soviets, the KAL 007 incident underscored both the Americans' antagonistic nature and the inadequacies of Soviet air defense.

General Secretary Yuri Andropov had concluded that the United States was actively preparing for war even before the KAL tragedy. In May 1981, while he was still director of the KGB, Andropov had announced at a major KGB conference, "There is now the possibility of a nuclear first strike." Henceforth, Andropov declared, the top priority for Soviet intelligence was the detection of the West's preparations for

---

42. Michael Mandelbaum, "The Luck of the President," 399.

43. Andrew and Gordievsky, *KGB,* 500; "Ideas," CBC, 9–10. During this period, the Soviet military was particularly influential in Soviet politics, and Soviet Defense Minister Dimitri Ustinov was especially so. See "Men of the Year," *Time,* January 2, 1984, 15; Shultz, *Turmoil and Triumph,* 478; and William Drozdiak, "Soviets' Switch Seen Reflecting Power Struggle," *Washington Post,* November 20, 1983.

attack. Toward this end the KGB would, for the first time, join together with the military intelligence agency, the GRU, in a global intelligence-gathering operation. The name of this program was "Raketno Yadernoye Napadenie" (RYAN), or "Nuclear Missile Attack."[44]

In late 1981 Moscow had begun sending its KGB offices telegrams outlining the early warning signals of a nuclear attack by the West, and requesting reports on the activities of Western officials and business people. KGB officials in London, for example, were required to monitor the activity at 10 Downing Street, the Ministry of Defense, the Foreign Offices, and the American embassy. Agents were to report every two weeks on the number of cars parked at these locations, the number of lights on inside, and any foot traffic. London officials were also required to make fortnightly reports on blood supplies and the price being paid for blood. (Moscow believed that the West would begin stockpiling blood in preparation for their nuclear attack, thus driving up the price paid for donations. Apparently, the Kremlin was not aware that British blood donors had not been paid since World War II.) Moscow also wanted its London KGB officers to cultivate relations with British bankers in the belief that "bankers would have some kind of advance warning because the nature of the capitalist system was such that the leading capitalists would be commissioned to try to keep some kind of a credit system going after the battle of Armageddon."[45]

These telegrams from Moscow increased in frequency throughout 1982. Oleg Gordievsky, a deputy KGB chief in London at the time, has recalled, "Yuri Andropov's election as General Secretary [in November 1982] gave added impetus to RYAN. . . . The workload . . . became staggering." Gordievsky added that Operation RYAN "created a vicious circle of intelligence collection and assessment."

> Because the political leadership was expecting to hear that the West was becoming more aggressive, more threatening, better armed, the KGB was obedient and reported: yes, the West was

44. Andrew and Gordievsky, *KGB*, 488; Brook-Shepherd, *Storm Birds*, 267; "Ideas," CBC, 1.
45. Brook-Shepherd, *Storm Birds*, 267; "Ideas," CBC, 6; Andrew and Gordievsky, *KGB*, 488–89.

arming . . . it may signify something sinister. And the reports of the military intelligence were worse, because, being more primitive and oriented toward military reporting, they exaggerated the Western military threat even more than the KGB did. . . . Residencies were, in effect, required to report alarming information even if they themselves were skeptical of it. The Centre was duly alarmed by what they reported and demanded more.[46]

Soviet intelligence agencies had spent two and a half years searching for evidence of an impending American nuclear attack. In November 1983 they thought they had found it.[47]

Moscow was distressed by numerous aspects of Able Archer 83. Its sheer scope was unprecedented, spanning from Norway to Turkey and westward to the Atlantic. Moreover, NATO's communications patterns and styles were new. The Kremlin had monitored NATO messages during military exercises before, but had never observed the procedures and formats the West was employing during Able Archer 83. Furthermore, during this exercise, NATO forces appeared to be on a higher alert status than was customary during war games.

Moscow's own war plans envisaged launching a nuclear attack under the camouflage of a planned exercise, and elements within Moscow feared NATO plans might be similar to their own. Consequently, on November 5 Moscow sent messages to its KGB residencies across Europe emphasizing the need for heightened surveillance. The telegram added, "Surprise is the key element in the main adversary's plans and preparations for war in today's conditions. As a result, it can be assumed that the period of time from the moment when the preliminary decision for RYAN is taken up to the order to deliver the strike will be of very short duration, possibly seven to ten days."[48] This time frame, of course, coincided with Exercise Able Archer.

46. Andrew and Gordievsky, *KGB*, 492–93; "Ideas," CBC, 2.

47. Even into the late 1980s powerful members of the Soviet defense establishment continued to believe that the United States was contemplating a nuclear first strike against the Soviet Union. See Stephen M. Meyer, "The Sources and Prospects of Gorbachev's New Political Thinking on Security," 137 n. 33.

48. Andrew and Gordievsky, *KGB*, 502; "Ideas," CBC, 10; Brook-Shepherd, *Storm Birds,* 270.

That same day Politburo member Grigory Vasilyevich Romanov addressed the Kremlin Palace of Congresses in order to commemorate the October Revolution. Romanov, who was considered to be a possible successor to General Secretary Andropov, remarked to the packed crowd,

> The development of events in the world arena demands from us the highest vigilance, restraint, firmness and unremitting attention to the strengthening of the country's defense capability. . . . Perhaps never before in the postwar decades has the situation in the world arena been as tense as it is now. . . . Comrades! The international situation at present is white hot, thoroughly white hot.[49]

American analysts, who were used to reading in between the lines of Soviet statements, were perplexed by these remarks. Unaware of Exercise Able Archer, Western observers were not sure why Romanov referred to the situation as "white hot." Many therefore dismissed the comments as Soviet propaganda. "No Russian dares accuse a man with such power . . . of engaging in hyperbole," Don Oberdorfer commented on the front page of *The Washington Post*. "But 'white hot' when there has been no overt act or threat of war? Is that how the Soviet leadership really sees the superpower rivalry . . . ?"[50]

Perhaps in a classic case of the "vicious circle of intelligence" that Oleg Gordievsky referred to, after receiving Moscow's flash telegram warning of a surprise attack, KGB agents subsequently reported a heightened state of alert at U.S. military bases in Europe. Two different groups of KGB agents monitoring American military bases in Germany erroneously reported that U.S. troops had been placed on alert. They also reported "changed patterns of officer movement and the observation by some bases of one hour's radio silence between 1800 and 1900 hours, Moscow time." Moscow immediately sent out

49. "Romanov Keynotes Nov. 7 Celebration," *CDSP*, 35:45, 5–6. The "white hot" comment was carried on the front page of both *Izvestia* and *Pravda* on November 6, 1983.

50. Don Oberdorfer, "War of Words," *Washington Post*, November 21, 1983. See also Murrey Marder, "Defector Told of Soviet Alert," *Washington Post*, August 8, 1986.

flash telegrams on November 8–9 to KGB and GRU residencies in Western Europe warning of the perceived state of alert at American military bases. Reminding officers of its own plans to launch a nuclear attack under the cover of a planned exercise, Moscow warned that Able Archer might be camouflaging Western preparations for a nuclear strike against the Soviet Union. The Kremlin instructed residencies to report as a matter of urgency on the reasons for the alert, and on any changes in other RYAN indicators.[51]

It was at this point that the situation became critical. Moscow knew that in the face of an impending nuclear strike against the Soviet Union, it had to prepare to launch its own nuclear weapons. Moscow's options were either to launch first in the hope of preempting a NATO strike, or to launch immediately after it was certain that NATO had begun its attack. If NATO and the Americans were going to unleash their nuclear weapons, as Soviet intelligence sources were indicating, then the Soviet Union would respond in kind. Therefore, in early November 1983 Moscow upgraded the alert status of twelve of its nuclear-capable fighter aircraft. In East Germany and in Poland, Soviet forces began to prepare for a retaliatory nuclear strike.[52]

"Operation Able Archer," author Christopher Andrew has remarked, "was probably the most dangerous moment that the world has lived through since the Cuban Missile Crisis in the autumn of 1962."[53] Subsequent remarks by Soviet Defense Minister Dimitri

51. Interviews with anonymous officials; Andrew and Gordievsky, *KGB,* 502–3; "Ideas," CBC, 10; Brook-Shepherd, *Storm Birds,* 270.

52. Interviews with anonymous officials; Oberdorfer, *The Turn,* 66.

53. "Ideas," CBC, 11. Interestingly, there was a spate of references to the Cuban Missile Crisis during November–December 1983. In a November 17 speech, French President François Mitterrand warned that "the present situation is comparable to the Cuban Missile Crisis" (Flora Lewis, "Missiles and Pacifists," *New York Times,* November 18, 1983). On November 23, 1983, the Soviet periodical *Literaturnaya Gazeta* ran a fictionalized recollection of the Cuban Missile Crisis causing American analysts to question its meaning (Hedrick Smith, "Andropov Is Spotted Being Driven to Work," *New York Times,* December 8, 1983, A8). On December 9, 1983, Senator Ted Kennedy, who was a member of the Senate Foreign Relations Committee, called for superpower dialogue, asserting that Soviet-American relations were "at the lowest point since the Cuban missile crisis. . . . We cannot afford to play U.S.-Russian roulette with the fate of the earth" (Hedrick Smith, "Reagan Finds a Lesser Evil in

Ustinov support Andrew's assertion. In a front page article in *Pravda* on November 19, 1983, Ustinov declared,

> The great Lenin taught us to raise our political and military vigilance, to strengthen our defensive might, and to always be on the alert. The Soviet people are drawing this conclusion today as well. Their Armed Forces are in constant readiness to administer a crushing rebuff to an aggressor. . . . The dangerous nature of the military exercises conducted by the US and NATO in recent years commands attention. These exercises are characterized by an enormous scope, and they are becoming increasingly difficult to distinguish from a real deployment of armed forces for aggression. NATO's Autumn Forge-83 maneuvers, which have just ended, involved 300,000 people and large amounts of arms and combat equipment. The area of maneuvers encompassed Western Europe, from Norway to Turkey, and included the Atlantic. . . . Are military exercises of this scope necessary for the normal training of troops? Of course not.[54]

Ultimately, Able Archer 83 ended on November 11, 1983, without incident. Prevailing nuclear doctrine at the time held that in the face of an impending nuclear attack, the Soviets should have sought to avoid disaster by launching a preemptive nuclear attack of their own. For reasons that remain unknown, they did not do this.

U.S. Response to Events Surrounding Able Archer 83

Reagan officials have sought to avoid discussing Able Archer publicly. It is clear, however, that they initially responded in disbelief to Moscow's reaction to the war game. Angelo Codevilla, who was an analyst for the United States Senate Select Committee on Intelligence

---

Indefinite Recess of Talks," *New York Times*, December 9, 1983). And in his January 16 address President Reagan recalled a statement by John F. Kennedy, "Let us not be blind to our differences, but let us also direct attention to our common interests and to the means by which those differences can be resolved." President Kennedy made those remarks at the conclusion of the Cuban Missile Crisis (Michael Getler, "Speech to Cite Buildup, Economy," *Washington Post*, January 16, 1984).

54. "Ustinov: USSR Will Counter Euromissiles," *CDSP,* 35:46, 6–7.

at the time, recollected, "When the report surfaced that the KGB was worried about an American first strike, there was a great deal of incredulity: How could anyone be this ignorant of America?" Shultz concurred, stating that the Soviet belief that the United States would launch a nuclear first strike "was incredible, at least to us."[55]

As intelligence officers passed more information to Washington, however, administration officials became increasingly concerned. In some respects, it was conceivable that Moscow could have misinterpreted the war game as preparation for a real nuclear attack. Relations between East and West were especially tense—this was why the exercise had been scaled back. Moreover, "false warning" incidents were not unknown. In the United States, there had been more than five such instances in the previous fourteen years. One of the more bizarre cases occurred during the height of the Cuban Missile Crisis in 1962. A sentry at a Minnesota military base mistook a bear climbing a fence for a possible saboteur, and triggered the sabotage alarm. However, at Volk Field in Wisconsin, the wrong alarm went off: the bell signaling that a nuclear war had begun. Since U.S. pilots had been told that there would be no drills during the crisis, they ran to their nuclear-armed aircraft believing that Armageddon was underway. As the pilots started their engines, the base commander discovered what had happened, and shouted to another to stop the deployment. The official jumped into a military vehicle and drove onto the runway flashing his lights as the pilots began taxiing for take-off. Fortunately, none of the planes had yet departed, and the mission was aborted.[56]

The sources of the information regarding the Soviet panic over Able Archer were highly credible, which added to the administration's growing concern. Much information came from Oleg Gordievsky, who, although he was the deputy chief of the KGB station in London, was working with the British intelligence agency, MI6. Gordievsky had passed along many Soviet documents that had proved valuable for the Western allies. The United States had scant information about the Soviet leadership, and the KGB official's reports gave Washington

55. "Ideas," CBC, 11; Shultz, *Turmoil and Triumph*, 464.
56. Scott Sagan, *The Limits of Safety: Organizations, Accidents, and Nuclear Weapons*, 3.

insight into Soviet strategic thinking and their paranoia regarding attack. "Gordievsky furnished a lot of good information," Weinberger has asserted; "he was credible." The CIA station in London also confirmed that the Soviets had been genuinely alarmed that the United States was preparing for a nuclear attack. This report was especially noteworthy because the CIA had been in the habit of portraying the Soviets as expansionist ideologues, not paranoiacs. A third report from an American in Eastern Europe substantiated that Moscow was alarmed. This source had connections to leading officials in the Soviet Union, and told Washington that Moscow truly feared that the West was preparing for a nuclear first strike.[57]

"The situation was very grave. It was serious," National Security Adviser McFarlane has recollected. "We were monitoring things very closely." Information about the incident was also highly classified. It was clear that the Soviets had panicked, but administration officials disagreed about the meaning of Moscow's actions. For example, Defense Secretary Weinberger "didn't give a great amount of credibility" to the Soviets' alarm. In his view, Moscow had feigned panic in order to play on White House fears about a nuclear accident or an inadvertent nuclear exchange. Secretary Shultz was also skeptical, believing that the "war scare" might simply have been part of a Soviet propaganda

57. Interviews with Weinberger, McFarlane, and other, anonymous, officials; Oberdorfer, *Turn*, 66. One of the most pressing problems facing Bill Casey when he took over as director of the CIA was the fact that the U.S. had virtually no human intelligence sources within the Politburo. See Woodward, *Veil*; and Aspin, "Misreading Intelligence." Without exception, all the individuals interviewed for this book attested to Gordievsky's credibility regarding Able Archer. Gordievsky defected in 1985, and soon after, the American government spent considerable time debriefing him and querying him about the Soviet leadership. In early October 1985, CIA Director Casey visited Gordievsky in Britain regarding the upcoming Geneva summit meeting. Gordievsky provided Casey with information on Gorbachev's policy views and his negotiating style, among other things. Around that time Gordievsky also prepared a fifty-page paper on Soviet thinking about international affairs for the American government. Entitled "Soviet Perceptions of Nuclear Warfare," this paper examined the psychology of the Kremlin's approach to nuclear strategy. In February 1986 Gordievsky was secretly brought to the Washington area for a series of meetings with the senior officials of the National Security Council, the State and Defense Departments, and U.S. intelligence agencies. See also Oberdorfer, *The Turn*, 66; and Shultz, *Turmoil and Triumph*, 507, 691, 864–65.

campaign aimed at creating tension within the Western alliance. Like the others, McFarlane could not bring himself to accept that the Soviets truly believed the West would launch a nuclear first strike against them. It made no sense, he argued. "[Soviet Foreign Minister] Andrei Gromyko knew us well enough to know that there was no way the U.S. could launch a first strike," he reasoned.[58]

President Reagan was not able to discount the Soviets' alarm as readily as his advisers did. According to McFarlane, the president responded with "genuine anxiety" to the news of the Soviet panic. Reagan was visibly shaken by the Soviets' misinterpretation of the NATO drill. The president had never believed that his war of words would lead to an armed conflict with the Soviet Union. More ominously, he had always felt that, in the face of an impending nuclear exchange, reason would not prevail. As he saw it, both sides "had many contingency plans for responding to a nuclear attack. But everything would happen so fast that I wondered how much planning or reason could be applied in such a crisis." Facing impending defeat, Reagan believed that a nation would "turn to the ultimate weapon." He also knew that preparations for a nuclear first strike against Moscow would have placed them in such a position.[59]

McFarlane told the president of his belief that Gromyko knew Washington was not capable of launching a nuclear first strike. Reagan considered this, but wondered whether General Secretary Andropov shared this understanding. Andropov, the impetus behind Operation RYAN, had no first-hand knowledge of the United States or the way its leaders thought. He also had a reputation for being paranoid about a U.S. strike. Even if Andropov did share his foreign minister's view, the president reasoned, "Gromyko and Andropov are just two players sitting on top of a large military machine." Reagan questioned whether the Politburo had the ability to stave off panic and miscalculation among the military officials who could actually launch the weapons.

58. Interviews with Weinberger, McFarlane, and anonymous officials; Shultz, *Turmoil and Triumph,* 464.

59. Interviews with McFarlane and anonymous officials; Reagan, *An American Life,* 257; Reagan, Remarks at Rancho del Cielo, August 13, 1981, *WCPD* 17:870; Reagan, News Conference, November 10, 1981, *WCPD* 17:1244.

The president feared that anxiety would override reason, resulting in a nuclear exchange that neither capital wanted. According to McFarlane, Reagan subsequently brought up the Armageddon story during a meeting with his senior advisers.[60]

On the day that Exercise Able Archer ended, November 11, 1983, President Reagan made his first public appeal for the total elimination of nuclear armaments in the world. In a speech to the Japanese Diet Reagan proclaimed, "I believe there can only be one policy for preserving our precious civilization in this modern age: a nuclear war can never be won and must never be fought. . . . I know I speak for people everywhere when I say our dream is to see the day when nuclear weapons will be banished from the face of the earth." The president repeated this call at a news conference on December 14, saying, "We must come to the realization that those weapons should be outlawed world-wide forever."[61]

Available evidence indicates, then, that the events surrounding Able Archer 83 caused President Reagan to reassess his approach to superpower relations and consequently to redirect U.S. policy toward Moscow. Ronald Reagan perceived Exercise Able Archer to be a nuclear "near-miss." Shortly before the exercise, he had been primed to think about nuclear annihilation. It was thus relatively easy for Reagan to reach his conclusion, especially given his abhorrence of nuclear weapons and his longstanding beliefs about nuclear Armageddon. Because the scenario of nuclear war readily available to Reagan, he estimated it more likely to happen. Therefore, when the president confronted ambiguous information about the Soviets' reaction to Able Archer, he assimilated it to the prime. Upon learning that Moscow had readied its nuclear-capable aircraft, the president interpreted this behavior as the beginning of an inadvertent nuclear exchange.

According to National Security Adviser McFarlane, the "war scare" had a "big influence" on Reagan's subsequent approach to the Soviet

60. Interviews with McFarlane; Oberdorfer, *The Turn,* 66.
61. Lou Cannon, "President Hails Japan as Partner," *Washington Post,* November 11, 1983; "Reagan Suggests Ending All Nuclear Arsenals," *Wall Street Journal,* December 15, 1983.

Union. The events surrounding Able Archer led the president to be less confrontational toward Moscow. Key sections of the president's turning-point address, which was delivered in January 1984, were meant to allay Soviet fears about the exercise. McFarlane, who helped draft the speech, notes that the president's references to "dangerous misunderstandings and miscalculations" referred to the Soviet response to the war game. In a thinly veiled statement, Reagan declared that he sought to find "meaningful ways to reduce the uncertainty and potential for misinterpretation surrounding military activities and to diminish the risk of surprise attack." Likewise, the president's assurances that the United States "poses no threat to the security of the Soviet Union" were meant to clarify U.S. intentions for the Kremlin. Reagan officials continued to repeat these themes throughout 1984 and 1985 in an effort to ensure that such a near-miss would not happen again.[62]

Without naming Exercise Able Archer, the president discusses in his memoirs the events of the fall of 1983 and the impact they had on his outlook.

> Three years had taught me something surprising about the Russians: Many people at the top of the Soviet hierarchy were genuinely afraid of America and Americans. Perhaps this shouldn't have surprised me, but it did. In fact, I had difficulty accepting my own conclusions at first. I'd always felt that from our deeds it must be clear to anyone that Americans were a moral people who starting at the birth of our nation had always used our power only as a force of good in the world. . . . During my first three years in Washington, I think many of us in the administration took it for granted that the Russians, like ourselves, considered it unthinkable that the United States would launch a first strike against them. But the more experience I had with Soviet leaders and [those] who knew them, the more I began to realize that many Soviet officials feared us not only as adversaries, but as

62. McFarlane interview, July 7, 1995; Reagan, "The U.S.-Soviet Relationship," *AFP:CD 1984*, 2–3. The following day Secretary Shultz had reiterated the "need to reduce the danger of surprise attack, miscalculation, or misunderstanding" between the superpowers. Shultz, Statement at the CDE, *DSB* (March 1984), 34.

potential aggressors who might hurl nuclear weapons at them in a first strike. . . . Well, if that was the case, I was even more anxious to get a top leader in a room alone and try to convince him we had no designs on the Soviet Union and the Russians had nothing to fear from us.[63]

Reagan learned that the Soviet leadership perceived him differently than he perceived himself. The Kremlin misunderstood the president's intentions. To Reagan's shock and disbelief, the Soviets believed that he would initiate a nuclear war against the USSR. This misperception, Reagan realized, had brought the world to the edge of a nuclear conflict. Consequently, in order to guard against an accidental nuclear exchange in the future, Reagan needed to correct Soviet misperceptions about American intentions. It became imperative to engage in a dialogue with the Soviets. At the same time, it was essential to reduce the number of nuclear arms in the world. Misunderstandings involving conventional weaponry would not be nearly as tragic as those involving nuclear armaments.

If one is to argue that President Reagan redirected U.S. Soviet policy because of a change in his own views, it would seem logical that the president would also take a more active role in the formulation of that policy. This is precisely what occurred. In late 1983 Ronald Reagan took the reins and began to redirect U.S. Soviet policy. A tragedy had narrowly been avoided, he believed, and changes needed to be instituted quickly.

Reagan's main goals were to foster dialogue and to reduce and ultimately eliminate nuclear arms. Within one week after the conclusion of Able Archer 83 the president established a small group within the National Security Planning Group to take control of relations with the Soviet Union, and to chart a course toward improved dialogue. In connection with this decision, Reagan remarked in his diary, "I feel the Soviets are so defense minded, so paranoid about being attacked that, without in any way being soft on them, we ought to tell them no one here has any intention of doing anything like that."[64] By the last week

63. Reagan, *An American Life*, 588–89.
64. Ibid., 589.

in November Assistant Secretary of State Richard Burt was devising a strategy for adopting a more conciliatory approach to Moscow. Shultz used Burt's recommendations as the basis for a presentation on U.S. Soviet policy to the president on December 16. The following day Reagan informed Shultz that he wanted to make a major speech on U.S.-Soviet relations, emphasizing the need for dialogue and his readiness to abolish nuclear weapons. By December 19 Reagan, Shultz, McFarlane, and Soviet expert Jack Matlock had written a first draft of what would come to be the president's January 16 address.[65]

Reagan continued to play an active role in the development of U.S. Soviet policy through the end of 1985. In early 1984 he became increasingly intent on holding a summit meeting with his Soviet counterpart. He met with President Mika Spiljak of Yugoslavia at the White House in early January and used the opportunity to learn more about the Soviet leadership and its politics. Spiljak, a former ambassador to the USSR, told Reagan that there was anxiety in Moscow over American intentions. The president noted in his diary after the meeting, "Spiljak confirmed some of my thoughts. . . . He believes that coupled with their expansionist philosophy, [the Kremlin] is also insecure and genuinely frightened of us." This further encouraged Reagan that a meeting was imperative.[66]

Eight weeks later, the president quizzed West German Chancellor Helmut Kohl about the Soviet leadership. Kohl's predecessor, Helmut Schmidt, had said repeatedly that the superpowers "were not in touch with each other's reality" and that "more human contact was necessary." Reagan wanted to see how his successor read the situation. Kohl urged the president to hold a summit meeting with General Secretary Chernenko. The Soviets were "motivated at least in part by insecurity and a suspicion that [the NATO] allies mean them harm," Kohl believed. A summit meeting could be a step toward alleviating these fears.[67]

By March 1984 Reagan had virtually excluded the foreign policy bureaucracy from the conduct of U.S.-Soviet relations. "Because arms

65. Oberdorfer, *The Turn*, 71; Matlock interview, September 19, 1995; McFarlane, *Special Trust*, 295; Shultz, *Turmoil and Triumph*, 376.

66. Reagan, *An American Life*, 589.

67. Shultz, *Turmoil and Triumph*, 5–6; Reagan, *An American Life*, 595.

reduction was so important," he commented, "I decided to switch to a more hands-on approach—without help from the bureaucrats." Reagan felt that the bureaucrats would slow the improvement of relations with the Soviet Union. Consequently, the president decided to communicate directly with General Secretary Chernenko. From that point on, Reagan consulted only with Vice President Bush, Weinberger, Shultz, and McFarlane on U.S. Soviet policy.[68]

In the summer of 1984 the president softened the conditions he had previously established in order for a summit meeting to take place and prepared for his first meeting with a high-level Soviet official. Reagan was to address the opening of the United Nations in September 1984 and had arranged to meet with Soviet Foreign Minister Andrei Gromyko at the White House four days later. The president was intent on distancing himself from his previously harsh rhetoric before his meeting with Gromyko. He rewrote several drafts of the UN speech prepared for him by his staff, softening its tone by removing all passages that could have been interpreted as accusatory. The president's call for greater cooperation between the two countries was expressed in very personal terms. "You know," he appeared to ad lib, "as I stand here and look out from this podium, there in front of me I can see the seat of the representative from the Soviet Union. And not far from that seat . . . is the seat of the representative of the United States. . . . In this historic assembly hall it is clear there's not a great distance between us. Outside this room, while there will still be clear differences, there is every reason why we should do all that is possible to shorten that distance."[69]

During Gromyko's visit on September 28, Reagan departed from previous practice by writing his own discussion points, rather than relying on the foreign policy bureaucracy's suggestions for the agenda of the meeting. The president also decided to expand his role in the negotiations. Previously, Reagan had habitually made the opening statement at such meetings and then turned the discussion over to

---

68. Reagan, *An American Life*, 594.

69. Cannon and Hoffman, "Soviet's Visit," *Washington Post*, September 30, 1984; "Holding Their Ground," *Time*, October 8, 1984, 19; Reagan, "Our Own Commitment to the Goals of the [UN] Charter Remain Steadfast," September 23, 1984, *AFP:CD 1984*, 224.

other administration officials. This time, according to one source who was present, "Reagan and Gromyko did nearly all the talking; their aides rarely got to say much." The president also insisted on a private meeting with Gromyko, without the presence of aides and staff. At that meeting Reagan claims that he "made it clear that we Americans have no hostile intentions toward his country and that we're not seeking military superiority."[70]

The president also became more involved in arms control negotiations than he had in the past, taking an active role in the preparations for the January 1985 meeting in Geneva between Shultz and Soviet Foreign Minister Gromyko. Beginning in the fall of 1984, Reagan actively participated in five full-scale meetings on arms control, discussing the intricacies of negotiating strategy. Remarked Don Oberdorfer, "This was an unusual amount of time and attention for a president who was so uninvolved several years earlier that he did not seem to know that the Soviets relied primarily on land-based missiles for their nuclear clout."[71]

Upon Chernenko's death in March 1985, Reagan issued a summit invitation to the new Soviet leader, Mikhail Gorbachev. The president has asserted that his fears about the reliance on nuclear weapons led him to extend this invitation. "I wanted to go to the negotiating table and end the madness of the MAD policy," Reagan remarked.

> I knew there were great differences between our two countries. Yet the stakes were too high for us not to try to find a common ground where we could meet and reduce the risk of Armageddon. . . . I sensed that [Gorbachev] was willing to listen and that possibly he sensed, as I did, that on both sides of the Iron Curtain there were myths and misconceptions that had contributed to misunderstandings and our potentially fatal mistrust of each other.[72]

70. "Holding Their Ground," *Time*, October 8, 1984, 17–19; and Cannon and Hoffman, "Soviet's Visit," *Washington Post*, September 30, 1984; Don Oberdorfer, "Reagan Promises Soviets 'Fair Deal,'" *Washington Post*, September 30, 1984.

71. Cannon and Hoffman, "Soviet's Visit," *Washington Post*, September 30, 1984; Oberdorfer, *The Turn*, 100.

72. Reagan, *An American Life*, 13–14.

Conclusion

In 1990 *Washington Post* correspondent Don Oberdorfer asked President Reagan why he thought U.S.-Soviet relations had improved so dramatically. Reagan responded that relations had improved because not one, but both, capitals had changed their approach to the superpower relationship. Because of the Soviet Union's economic weakness Gorbachev had needed to divert resources away from the military sector, the president asserted. This led to a change in Moscow's approach to superpower relations. However, Reagan did not point to Gorbachev's revolutionary politics as the reason for the change in American policy. The changes in U.S. policy had different roots. "[I felt that] it was a danger," the president confided, "to have a world so heavily armed that one misstep could trigger a great war." Reagan's fear of an accidental war, he asserted, caused him to redirect U.S. Soviet policy.[73]

The "leader-driven" hypothesis satisfies the three criteria established at the outset of the book for evaluating competing explanations of policy change. It explains the catalyst for the shift in policy. Events during the fall of 1983 caused Reagan to reassess and revise his understanding of both the Kremlin and superpower relations. He learned that Moscow perceived him far differently than he perceived himself: Soviet leaders feared that Reagan would initiate a nuclear first strike against them. Thus, their actions were not solely motivated by a communist desire to foster global revolution. Rather, the Kremlin sought to protect itself against nuclear annihilation. The president understood, and shared, such fears. After standing on the brink of what he believed could have been an inadvertent nuclear exchange, he concluded that the main threat to U.S. security was not the Soviet Union, but rather, nuclear weapons themselves. Washington and Moscow shared a common enemy—the possibility of an inadvertent nuclear holocaust.

As president, Reagan had the capacity to redirect U.S. policy according to his new views. As the preeminent authority in U.S. foreign

73. Oberdorfer, *The Turn*, 438.

policy, he had the authority to speak for the nation.[74] Weinberger, Casey, and Meese disagreed with the more conciliatory posture, but their protestations had little effect. Within the executive branch, Reagan's view was the only one that mattered.

This hypothesis also explains the timing of the policy shift. As noted earlier, U.S. policy changed within a ten-week window. On October 31, 1983, Deputy Secretary of State Ken Dam had given a speech that epitomized the Reagan administration's early hard-line position toward Moscow. On January 16, 1984, the president delivered his turning-point address. Exercise Able Archer took place within this window. The war game began two days after Dam's speech, and concluded on November 11—the same day that the president began publicly calling for the total elimination of nuclear armaments throughout the globe. Within a week after Able Archer ended, foreign policy making had been restructured and a task force had been established with the sole mission of opening dialogue with the Kremlin. By mid-December drafts of Reagan's turning-point address were being circulated through Washington's upper echelons.

The leader-driven explanation also clarifies why U.S. policy changed in the manner it did. The Reagan administration began pursuing "cooperation and understanding" with the Soviet Union in 1984 because it sought to avoid inadvertent nuclear exchanges in the future. It sought to defuse the tension that had nearly led to an accidental nuclear exchange and to convince the Kremlin of the superpowers' common interest in removing the threat of nuclear annihilation. The events of the autumn of 1983 also caused Reagan officials to place greater emphasis on arms reduction. As long as there were nuclear weapons, there was the threat of nuclear war, whether it be an intentional or an inadvertent war. Moreover, it became "imperative" for the superpowers to engage in dialogue because lack of communication had nearly resulted in catastrophe. Reagan needed to assure the Kremlin that Washington was not planning a nuclear first strike against them. He also needed to correct Moscow's "dangerous misunderstandings" about his intentions.

74. See *The United States v Curtiss-Wright Export Corporation* 299 US 304 (1936).

Thus, the evidence suggests that President Reagan was responsible for the dramatic and abrupt reversal in U.S. Soviet policy. Reagan redirected U.S. policy in response to his own changing views about the Soviet leadership. Far from being a "passive president," Reagan took charge and reversed Washington's confrontational approach to Moscow. The president himself placed the United States on the path toward a rapprochement with the Soviet Union.

6

Conclusions

THIS BOOK BEGAN BY CHALLENGING the conventional wisdom regarding the Reagan administration's role in ending the cold war. Both liberals and conservatives alike have contended that the Reagan administration became more conciliatory toward the Soviet Union only *after* Moscow had begun to reform. In the liberal view, Reagan was a "lucky bumbler." The president was simply the person who happened to be occupying the Oval Office when the Soviets decided to end the cold war. In this view, Reagan changed his policy in response to Mikhail Gorbachev's personal charms. Captivated by Gorbachev's engaging personality, and impressed by his early reforms, the president simply followed Gorbachev's lead.

Conservatives also suggest that Reagan responded to changes within the USSR, although their reasoning is much different. In this view the Reagan administration's hard-line policy and military buildup placed enormous pressure on the Soviet Union. These policies forced Gorbachev to realize that his country could no longer afford to engage in a costly arms race or to maintain spheres of influence. Therefore, the Soviet leader began to seek an end to superpower hostilities. The Reagan administration only became more conciliatory once it was clear that the Kremlin had conceded the cold war.

In short, both schools of thought have argued that the Reagan administration played a reactive role in ending the cold war: Washington became more conciliatory only in response to changes within the Soviet Union.

This study contends that the Reagan administration began seeking a rapprochement with Moscow *before* the Soviets began to reform. Beginning in January 1984 Washington actively sought to improve superpower relations—despite the fact that Yuri Andropov and his old-school comrades still dominated the Politburo. The reversal in U.S. policy preceded *glasnost* and *perestroika* by more than two years. Therefore, both the liberal and the conservative views on the ending of the cold war are inaccurate. Reagan was not simply lucky enough to be in the right place at the right time. Beginning in late 1983, the president actively sought to reduce superpower hostilities. Reagan ardently pursued a rapprochement with the Soviets. But the view that Reagan pursued a hard-line policy until the Soviets capitulated is equally erroneous. Reagan abandoned his confrontational posture at a time when the Soviets were still fighting the cold war. It could be argued, then, that Reagan blinked first.

For a number of reasons, the 1984 reversal in U.S. policy can be interpreted as the beginning of the end of the cold war. For one thing, it introduced a shift in Washington's approach to Moscow. The Reagan administration now actively sought cooperation and understanding between the superpowers. Washington sought to engage Moscow rather than to condemn it. The policy shift also set into motion a variety of activities that would lead to further improvements in superpower relations. The initiatives introduced in 1984 had a snow-ball effect. For example, in 1984 the administration began seeking a superpower summit meeting. These efforts led to the 1985 meeting in Geneva between Reagan and Gorbachev. The Geneva summit, in turn, led to further meetings in Reykjavik, Moscow, and Washington. Finally, the 1984 policy shift signaled Washington's willingness to be more receptive to Soviet efforts to improve bilateral relations. The shift in Reagan's thinking meant that Washington would be more receptive to Gorbachev's "new thinking." If the United States had not changed course in 1984, it is likely that the Reagan administration would have been far more skeptical of Gorbachev's early reforms. One can only wonder whether the progress that was made during the Reagan-Gorbachev years would have occurred in the absence of the previous reversal in U.S. policy.

None of this is meant to suggest that the Reagan administration planned the end of the cold war, however. The White House sought to improve relations, but it is doubtful that anyone within the adminis-tration envisioned the momentous events of the late 1980s. Moreover, Gorbachev's role in bringing about the end of the cold war cannot be overstated. The manner in which he revolutionized Soviet politics, particularly Soviet foreign policy, was pivotal.

The primary aim of this book has been to determine why the Reagan administration chose to reverse its Soviet policy in January 1984. Thus, it is a study of one case of self-correcting foreign policy change. It has drawn upon the rather limited existing literature on policy change in an effort not only to determine why the Reagan administration reversed course, but also to study foreign policy change more generally.

Drawing upon work by Charles Hermann and others, I have established a framework for systematically comparing competing explanations of foreign policy change. Scholars have posited four possible sources of foreign policy change: a shift in the international distribution of capabilities, a shift in public opinion, bureaucratic advocacy, and changes in an authoritative leader's views. In order to determine which of these explanations best explains the reversal in U.S. Soviet policy, each was evaluated according to the same three criteria: whether it explained (1) the catalyst for the change, (2) the timing of the shift, and (3) the nature of the policy changes.

Although conclusions are necessarily tentative, it is unlikely that shifts in the international distribution of military capabilities brought about the changes in the Reagan administration's Soviet policy. The relative balance of power had shifted back and forth for decades, yet the United States had continued to fight the cold war. Moreover, such an explanation does not explain why the administration reversed course within a span of ten weeks, or why certain themes came to dominate the administration's new policy.

While the hypothesis that public opinion forced the administration to reverse its hard-line policy during an election year seems plausible at first, it fails to satisfy any of the three criteria. According to this hypothesis, the catalyst for the policy reversal was a shift in U.S. public opinion, with a growing number of Americans seeking a more moderate approach to Moscow. However, evidence from polls does not support this allegation. Public approval of Reagan's hard-line policy had been growing throughout 1983. This explanation also suggests that the timing of the policy shift can be explained by the 1984 presidential election: Reagan reversed course in 1984 because he was trying to win reelection. While such an argument is plausible, the fact that Reagan delivered his speech at ten o'clock in the morning, when few American voters could hear it, suggests that there were other reasons for the timing of the policy change. Finally, this domestic politics explanation does not explain why U.S. policy changed in the manner it did. It is unable to spell out why the administration chose to reverse course rather than to simply modify its existing policy. It also cannot explain the administration's sudden interest in dialogue, its references to "dangerous misunderstandings," or why, after repeatedly scoffing at the idea that the Kremlin might feel threatened by the United States, Reagan officials suddenly began repeating that the United States "posed no threat to the security of the Soviet Union."

The bureaucratic advocacy explanation for the change in U.S. Soviet policy—the idea that Secretary of State Shultz and National Security Adviser McFarlane might have redirected U.S. Soviet policy in a manner more to their liking—is also not convincing. It requires one to accept that the weaker moderate faction within the administration, composed of relative newcomers, was able to overrule the dominant hard-line faction. The relative power of the moderate and hard-line factions indicates that U.S. Soviet policy should have continued to be confrontational. The fact that U.S. policy became more conciliatory suggests that someone with more authority than these officials stepped in. Moreover, this explanation was silent as to why the administration reversed course when it did. It could not explain the timing of the policy change. Finally, such a view does not entirely explain why U.S. policy changed in the manner it did. Granted, some of the changes introduced in January 1984 can plausibly be linked to Shultz's and McFarlane's more moderate views about superpower relations and arms control. However, the urgency surrounding the need for a summit, the references to "dangerous misunderstandings," and the repeated assurances that Washington did not threaten Moscow remain unexplained.

The leader-driven explanation is thus the most explanatory. In this view, President Reagan redirected U.S. policy in response to his own changing views about the Kremlin and superpower relations. This explanation posits that the catalyst for the policy change was Able Archer 83 and that the events surrounding the exercise forced

Reagan to confront his fears about nuclear war and to realize that the Kremlin misunderstood U.S. intentions. The incident also led the president to conclude that both superpowers faced a common enemy: an inadvertent nuclear holocaust. These realizations caused Reagan to revise his images of the Kremlin and of superpower relations and, consequently, to redirect U.S. policy in line with these new views. Such an explanation also explains the timing of the policy reversal: Exercise Able Archer occurred within the ten weeks between the administration's last hard-line speech and the president's January 1984 turning-point address. Most importantly, this hypothesis explains the nature of the policy changes. It spells out why the Reagan administration's policy goals and strategies changed in the way they did. It also explains the references to "dangerous misunderstandings," the repeated assurances that the United States "posed no threat" to Moscow, and the contention that there was an "imperative" need for dialogue.

In essence, this study suggests that Reagan "learned" while in office, and that, as president, he used his authority to translate his learning experience into official policy. He "learned" in that new experiences caused him to revise his understanding of the Soviet leadership and the superpower relationship.

An important caveat must be added, however. Reagan changed his image of the Kremlin—but he did not revise his assessment of communism. Through the end of his term in office, Reagan continued to believe that communism was a morally bankrupt ideology. For example, even after he had reversed his Soviet policy, the president continued to pursue the Reagan Doctrine, in which the United States actively supported anticommunist forces in less-developed countries. Pursuing a rapprochement with the Soviets on the one hand, and the Reagan Doctrine on the other, appears contradictory, but it is explicable. For one thing, Reagan's "logic" was frequently contradictory—and it never seemed to bother him. His interpretation of the Armageddon story is one example. If it was preordained that the world would end in a nuclear holocaust, it made no sense for the Reagan administration to spend billions of dollars developing SDI in an effort to protect Americans against such a calamity. The president ignored this contradiction. Moreover, according to Reagan's interpretation of the parable, a leader from the West would vanquish the Soviets in a great battle, after which the Western leader would be revealed as the Antichrist. If this were the case, then Reagan himself was the Antichrist. Although some liberals might have jokingly agreed with this characterization, it is doubtful that the president viewed it this way.

Cognitive psychology can also help to explain the apparent contradiction in Reagan's views about the Soviet leaders, on the one hand, and communism, on the other. Psychological studies would suggest that through his experience with Able Archer, the president became more "cognitively complex." That is, he began to differentiate the Soviet leadership from "communists" more generally. Thus, he saw Soviet leaders as a special case of communists; although they were part of a communist government, these men shared Reagan's concerns about international security and nuclear war. It was on the basis of these shared concerns that the president could engage with his Soviet counterparts. Such thinking explains the administration's new understanding of the superpower relationship: one based on a combination of rivalry and common interests.[1]

In this case, it was crucial that the person doing the learning was in a position to influence official policy. As president, Ronald Reagan was the preeminent authority in determining U.S. foreign policy. He had the power to redirect policy so as to coincide with his changing views.[2] Generally speaking, however, individual learning is neither a necessary nor a sufficient cause for policy change. Governments may change their foreign policies in the absence of learning. For example, they may modify their positions in order to appeal to public opinion or in response to congressional criticism. On the other hand, even when learning has occurred, it is not always certain that such learning will be translated into official policy. It very much depends on who has

1. There are a number of different approaches to cognitive complexity. For example, see Tetlock, "Learning in U.S. and Soviet Foreign Policy," 32–35; Stein, "Cognitive Psychology and Political Learning," 223–58; and Steven Weber, "Interactive Learning in U.S.-Soviet Arms Control," 784–824.

2. Of course, the president does not have total power over foreign policy making. On presidential power over foreign policy, see Arthur M. Schlesinger Jr., *The Imperial Presidency*; Harold Hongju Koh, *The National Security Constitution: Sharing Power after the Iran-Contra Affair*; and Louis Henkin, *Foreign Affairs and the Constitution*.

done the learning and whether that individual or group are able to affect policy outcomes.

Even though Reagan had much power over foreign policy, it is certain that other factors made it easier for him to reverse course. For example, Shultz and McFarlane had long favored a more conciliatory approach, and were therefore receptive to Reagan's changing views. Alexander Haig and William Clark might well have tried to dissuade the president from changing course. Likewise, some of Reagan's campaign advisers believed that a more moderate policy would aid the president's reelection campaign. These officials would also have been receptive to a policy shift, regardless of its source. The fact that many members of Congress were calling for a less confrontational posture toward Moscow also made it easier for Reagan to change his policy. The president could be assured that these congresspeople would support him once he began seeking a rapprochement.[3] In addition, a number of West European leaders had been lobbying the administration to be "less shrill" toward the Kremlin. These allies would also be supportive of a policy shift.[4] In short, there was a variety of constituencies that favored a more conciliatory policy, and this made it more politically acceptable for Reagan to implement such a change. However, this is not to suggest that these factors *caused* the policy change. There is little available evidence to suggest that these constituencies actually brought about the change in policy. They had been in place for years, pressuring Reagan to be less confrontational. U.S. policy toward Moscow had remained hard-line, however. But these other factors made it easier for Reagan to *implement* the changes.

This study finds, then, that a learning theory approach is most useful in explaining this case of self-correcting policy change. It is only through examining the president's changing views that one can understand why U.S. policy changed in the manner it did. However, learning theory must be applied carefully, and within certain lim-

3. In 1982, 28 senators and 154 representatives in Congress introduced two bipartisan resolutions calling for a nuclear freeze. See Bernard Gwertzman, "State Dept. Calls Arms Freeze Plan 'Dangerous' to U.S."; and John M. Goshko, "Reagan Will Endorse Nuclear Talks," *Washington Post,* March 29, 1982.

4. McFarlane interview, July 7, 1995.

itations. As noted, learning is neither a necessary nor a sufficient cause for policy change. Learning can only explain some cases of foreign policy change. Political scientists must therefore take care that learning theory approaches are used in conjunction with other explanations for policy change. That is, one can conclude that a learning theory explanation is most satisfactory only after comparing it to competing explanations of policy change. To argue that learning caused a policy shift without examining the explanatory power of competing explanations, as many analysts have done, is methodologically unsound.

Moreover, it is doubtful that political scientists will be able to develop "grand theories" of learning that will be able to explain a wide range of cases across various states and cultures. Learning has been defined in many different ways by many different scholars. For example, some argue that learning has occurred when governments are able to match ends to means more efficiently. Others define learning as changes in institutional procedures and organizational norms. Another school of thought argues that learning occurs not at the governmental level, but at the individual level. In this view, learning entails a change in a policy maker's "belief system," or "operational code." Still others maintain that learning entails an increase in "cognitive complexity." That is, learning has occurred when a policy maker's knowledge is organized in a more complex fashion.[5] While all these schools claim to study the effect of "learning" on politics,

5. On the efficiency conception of learning, see Tetlock, "Learning in U.S. and Soviet Foreign Policy," 35–38; Wallace J. Thies, "Learning in U.S. Policy toward Europe"; and Deborah Welch Larson, "Learning in U.S.-Soviet Relations: The Nixon-Kissinger Structure of Peace." On the organizational conception of learning, see Tetlock, "Learning in U.S. and Soviet Foreign Policy," 22; Etheredge, "Government Learning"; Coit D. Blacker, "Learning in the Nuclear Age: Soviet Strategic Arms Control Policy, 1969–1989"; and Franklyn Griffiths, "Attempted Learning: Soviet Policy toward the United States in the Brezhnev Era," 663–68. On the belief system conception of learning, see, for example, George, *Presidential Decisionmaking*; Jonathan Haslam, "Soviet Policy toward Western Europe since World War II"; and Tetlock, "Learning in U.S. and Soviet Foreign Policy," 27–31. Regarding cognitive complexity, see Tetlock, "Learning in U.S. and Soviet Foreign Policy," 32–35; Stein, "Cognitive Psychology and Political Learning," 223–58; and Weber, "Interactive Learning," 784–824.

each is actually studying a different phenomenon from the others. The efficiency theorists focus on the governmental level of analysis, and are interested in the allocation of resources. Organizational theorists also focus on the governmental level, yet they are interested in how standard operating procedures are modified. Those who study operational codes focus on leaders' beliefs. And those who focus on cognitive complexity are interested not in what a policy maker believes, but in how she intellectually organizes the world around her. In short, a variety of different phenomena have been lumped together under the rubric of "learning." While this study does not argue that one definition is superior to the others, it does contend that analysts must take care not to mix apples with oranges. That is, conclusions from studies in which learning is conceptualized as an increase in cognitive complexity should not be conflated with results from studies in which learning is defined as a more efficient matching of means to ends. Grand theories of learning cannot be inferred from these disparate studies.

This case raises another problem with the existing literature on learning and foreign policy making. For the most part, political scientists have approached the concept of learning from a purely cognitive perspective. Learning, it is assumed, is an entirely intellectual matter. But this study indicates that there can be an emotional component to learning. It suggests that fear can induce learning. Reagan did not learn anything in 1983 that he had not already been told. For years various experts had been advising the president that the Kremlin felt threatened by the West. For example, Shultz had shared his views that the Nazi invasion of the USSR during World War II had left a powerful psychological scar on the USSR. The secretary believed that Moscow feared another violation of its borders and tried to convince Reagan of the importance of these fears. Likewise, Soviet expert Jack Matlock had been writing briefs for the president about the Soviet leadership and the way in which it viewed superpower relations. Other advocates, such as Dr. Helen Caldicott, had met with Reagan to advise him of the dangers of nuclear weapons generally and the threat of an accidental nuclear exchange in particular. In short, for years various authorities had tried to instruct Reagan about the Soviet leaders and nuclear strategy. But these "lessons" had had little effect. This raises the question of why the president would discount certain lessons in one context, yet embrace them in another. Why did Reagan learn these lessons in late 1983, rather than earlier? The president's fear, it would seem, was a critical factor. Confronting the reality of his fears about nuclear war—looking into the nuclear abyss—was crucial. Nuclear fears brought about nuclear learning.[6]

Psychologists have long suspected that there is an affective, or emotional, component to cognition. There is increasing evidence that the ability to think "rationally" is dependent in large part upon one's feelings. "Emotions are an integral part of the ability to reason," recent psychological studies have concluded. "While too much emotion can impair reasoning, a lack of emotion can be equally harmful. Likewise, gut feelings and intuition are indispensable tools for rational decision making; without them humans would have great difficulty thinking about the future."[7]

The political science literature, on the other hand, has largely failed to consider the emotional component of learning. An exception is James G. Blight's *The Shattered Crystal Ball: Fear and Learning in the Cuban Missile Crisis*. A psychologist by training, Blight has reassessed decision making during the missile crisis and maintains that nuclear fears led to learning during the fall of 1962. The Cuban Missile Crisis was resolved peacefully, he argues, because United States and Soviet leaders' fears of an inadvertent nuclear holocaust led them to revise their stereotypes of each other and to conclude that superpower collaboration was imperative. Blight demonstrates that as the crisis was reaching its climax, U.S. policy makers feared that events would spin out of control, thus leading to a nuclear exchange that neither side wanted. Intentions would have no bearing on outcomes. "[During] the missile crisis the enemy shifted from the nuclear adversary to the nuclear 'environment,' " Blight contends.

6. Author interviews with Matlock and other, anonymous, officials; Shultz, *Turmoil and Triumph,* 117–19; Reagan, *An American Life,* 566.

7. Science journalist Sandra Blakeslee, reviewing a number of recent studies on the neural connections between emotion and reason ("Tracing the Brain's Pathways for Linking Emotion and Reason," *New York Times,* December 6, 1994). See also Antonio R. Damasio, *Descartes' Error: Emotion, Reason, and the Human Brain;* and Daniel Goleman, *Emotional Intelligence.*

"Feared nuclear inadvertence was in that instance the fear of a process and an outcome that was abhorred by both sides, thus creating a de facto, but powerful, common enemy against which both sides must unite. . . ." For President Kennedy, the realization that he would be responsible for such a nuclear holocaust was crucial and facilitated his learning. "As the crisis evolved," Blight asserts,

> the participants engaged in less stereotypical thinking [and] increased empathy with the plight of the adversary. . . . Leaders became obsessed with how their actions would be perceived by the adversary. . . . The reason for this preoccupation: both sides believed control was slipping away, both sides began to experience viscerally their absolute vulnerability to holocaust, and thus, both sides came to finally appreciate their identical nuclear predicaments. . . . This seems to me, more than anything else, to explain the peaceful resolution: a growing tacit understanding of the mutuality of shared nuclear danger.[8]

Harvard political scientist Joseph Nye admits in the foreword to Blight's book that he was initially skeptical of the psychologist's thesis. He is now convinced, however, of the pivotal role that fear played in nuclear learning during the Cuban Missile Crisis. "I am now compelled," Nye writes, "by his argument that in the deepest nuclear crisis leaders were fearful; that their fear was of losing control of events; that this fear seems to have led to learning that produced a peaceful resolution; and finally, that this cluster of factors is likely to be salient if we ever again face a crisis as dangerous as that of October 1962."[9]

The present study suggests that in 1983 the U.S. president faced an analogous situation, and that he did, in fact, experience many of the same emotions and concerns that leaders experienced during the Cuban Missile Crisis. Again, events seemed to be evading control. Again, it seemed as though intentions would have no bearing on outcomes. And once again, leaders were forced to confront their common

8. Blight, *Shattered Crystal Ball*, 161–63.
9. Nye, foreword to Blight, *Shattered Crystal Ball*, xviii.

vulnerability to an inadvertent nuclear exchange. Just as Kennedy had revised his stereotype about the Kremlin after the peaceful conclusion of the Cuban Missile Crisis, Reagan amended his image of the Soviet leaders in response to Able Archer. Kennedy abandoned his hard-line approach toward the Soviets in late 1962. Likewise, Reagan reversed his belligerent posture toward the Kremlin in late 1983. Interestingly, in drafting his turning-point address Reagan returned to the Cuban Missile Crisis, and borrowed a passage from a speech that Kennedy had delivered not long after that crisis had been resolved. "Let us not be blind to our differences," Reagan echoed Kennedy, "but let us direct attention to our common interests, and to solving our differences."[10]

It follows, then, that political scientists, when seeking to open up the black box of foreign policy decision making, should open up the box all the way: that is, greater consideration should be given to the impact that emotions can have on cognition.

One final note is in order. It has become customary to dismiss Ronald Reagan as a weak chief executive who let others within his administration develop and execute policy. In this view, Reagan was simply the spokesperson for the conservative coterie running the White House. This caricature of the president gained momentum during the Iran-contra affair and undoubtedly allowed him to emerge from that scandal relatively unscathed. But this study does not support such a docile characterization of the president. Rather, it suggests that Reagan had the capacity to be assertive and tenacious when developing foreign policy. For example, the president often rejected his officials' advice regarding arms control, an area that he admittedly knew little about. Reagan opposed the doctrine of mutual assured destruction despite the fact that almost all of his advisers, and his good friend Margaret Thatcher, supported it. He also initiated SDI and called for the reduction of nuclear armaments at a time when such ideas seemed far-fetched, even to his own officials. Reagan also opposed the idea of a nuclear freeze despite the fact that eighty percent of Americans favored such a proposal. The president could be equally tenacious regarding the administration's approach to Moscow.

10. Reagan, "The U.S.-Soviet Relationship," *AFP:CD 1984*, 406–11.

In 1982 he rejected Secretary Shultz's pleas that the president attend the funeral of General Secretary Brezhnev. The following year Reagan nixed Shultz's trip to Moscow to meet with Yuri Andropov, during which the secretary had hoped to lay the groundwork for a summit meeting. In early 1983 the president rejected out of hand his campaign handlers' suggestion that he change his Soviet policy so as to cater to public opinion. When it came to matters of principle, or issues that especially interested him, President Reagan could be resolute. Relations with the Soviet Union became just such an issue. In this case, Reagan took the reins of U.S. Soviet policy and redirected it. Moreover, he reversed course despite the fact that many of his trusted advisers opposed such a shift and despite the fact that he risked alienating his conservative supporters during an election year. These actions do not paint a portrait of a "passive president." Just as historians have revised their initial belief that Dwight Eisenhower was a spectator during his presidency, this study suggests that it is time to reconsider the Reagan legacy.

Bibliography

Abelson, Robert P., and Ariel Levi. "Decision Making and Decision Theory." In *Handbook of Social Psychology,* ed. G. Lindzey and E. Aronson. Vol. 1. New York: Random House, 1985.

American Foreign Policy: Current Documents [AFP:CD], 1981–1985. Washington, D.C.: U.S. Government Printing Office.

Anderson, Martin. *Revolution.* New York: Harcourt Brace Jovanovich, 1987.

Andrew, Christopher, and Oleg Gordievsky. *KGB: The Inside Story.* London: Hodder and Stoughton, 1990.

Aspin, Les. "Misreading Intelligence." *Foreign Policy* 43 (1981): 166–72.

Ball, Desmond, and Robert C. Toth. "Revising the SIOP: Taking War-Fighting to Dangerous Extremes." *International Security* 14 (1990): 69–89.

Beilenson, Laurence. *The Treaty Trap: A History of the Performance of Political Treaties by the United States and European Nations.* Washington, D.C.: Public Affairs Press, 1969.

Bialer, Seweryn, and Joan Afferica. "Reagan and Russia." *Foreign Affairs* 61 (Winter 1982–1983): 249–71.

Bialer, Seweryn, and Michael Mandelbaum, eds. *Gorbachev's Russia and American Foreign Policy.* Boulder, Colo.: Westview, 1988.

Blacker, Coit D. "Learning in the Nuclear Age: Soviet Strategic Arms Control Policy, 1969–1989." In *Learning in U.S. and Soviet Foreign Policy,* ed. G. W. Breslauer and P. E. Tetlock, 429–68. Boulder, Colo.: Westview, 1991.

Blight, James G. *The Shattered Crystal Ball: Fear and Learning in the Cuban Missile Crisis.* Lanham, Md.: Rowman and Littlefield, 1992.

Breslauer, George W. "What Have We Learned about Learning?" In *Learning in U.S. and Soviet Foreign Policy,* ed. G. W. Breslauer and P. E. Tetlock, 825–56. Boulder, Colo.: Westview, 1991.

Breslauer, George W., and Philip E. Tetlock, eds. *Learning in U.S. and Soviet Foreign Policy.* Boulder, Colo.: Westview, 1991.

Brook-Shepherd, Gordon. *The Storm Birds.* London: Weidenfeldt Nicolson, 1988.

Brown, Seyom. *The Faces of Power: United States Foreign Policy From Truman to Clinton.* New York: Columbia University Press, 1994.

Brownstein, Ronald, and Nina Easton. *Reagan's Ruling Class: Portraits of the President's Top 100 Officials.* Washington, D.C.: Presidential Accountability Group, 1982.

Caldwell, Lawrence T., and Robert Legvold. "Reagan through Soviet Eyes." *Foreign Policy* 52 (1983): 3–21.

Cannon, Lou. *President Reagan: The Role of a Lifetime.* New York: Simon and Schuster, 1991.

Carroll, John S. "The Effect of Imagining an Event on Expectations of the Event: An Interpretation in Terms of the Availability Heuristic." *Journal of Experimental Social Psychology* 14 (1978): 88–96.

Cortright, David. *Peace Works: The Citizen's Role in Ending the Cold War.* Boulder, Colo.: Westview, 1993.

Current Digest of the Soviet Press [CDSP]. Columbus, Ohio: Current Digest of the Soviet Press, 1981–1984.

Dallin, Alexander. *Black Box.* Berkeley and Los Angeles: University of California Press, 1985.

————. "Learning in U.S. Policy toward the Soviet Union in the 1980s." In *Learning in U.S. and Soviet Foreign Policy,* ed. G. W. Breslauer and P. E. Tetlock, 400–428. Boulder, Colo.: Westview, 1991.

————, and Gail W. Lapidus. "Reagan and the Russians: American Policy toward the Soviet Union." In *Eagle Resurgent?: The Reagan Era in American Foreign Policy,* ed. Kenneth A. Oye, R. J. Lieber, and D. Rothchild. Boston: Little, Brown and Company, 1987.

Damasio, Antonio R. *Descartes' Error: Emotion, Reason, and the Human Brain.* New York: Avon Books, 1994.

Deaver, Michael. *Behind the Scenes.* New York: William Morrow, 1987.

Deibel, Terry. "Reagan's Mixed Legacy." *Foreign Policy* 75 (1989): 34–55.

Department of State Bulletin [DSB], January 1981–December 1985. Washington, D.C.: U.S. Government Printing Office.

Destler, I. M., Leslie H. Gelb, and Anthony Lake. *Our Own Worst Enemy: The Unmaking of American Foreign Policy.* New York: Simon and Schuster, 1984.

Draper, Theodore. *A Very Thin Line: The Iran-Contra Affairs.* New York: Simon and Schuster, 1991.

————. "Revelations of the North Trial." *New York Review of Books,* August 17, 1989, 54–57.

Etheredge, Lloyd S. *Can Governments Learn?* New York: Pergamon Press, 1985.

————. "Government Learning: An Overview." In *Handbook of Political Behavior,* ed. Samuel Long, 73–155. New York: Plenum Press, 1981.

Feldman, Stanley, and Lee Sigelman. "The Political Impact of Prime-Time Television: 'The Day After.'" *The Journal of Politics* 47 (1985): 556–78.

Finlay, D. J., O. R. Holsti, and R. R. Fagen. *Enemies in Politics.* Chicago: Rand McNally, 1967.

Fisher, Louis. *Presidential War Power.* Lawrence: University Press of Kansas, 1995.

Fiske, Susan T., and Shelley E. Taylor. *Social Cognition.* New York: McGraw-Hill, 1991.

Fitzsimmons, Stephen J., and Hobart G. Osburn. "The Impact of Social Issues and Public Affairs Television Documentaries." *Public Opinion Quarterly* 32 (1968): 379–97.

Friedrich, Otto. "The View From the Street Corner." *Time,* January 2, 1984, 31.

Gaddis, John Lewis. "The Reagan Administration and Soviet American Relations." In *Reagan and the World,* ed. D. E. Kyvig, 17–38. New York: Praeger, 1990.

The Gallup Poll: Public Opinion 1983–1984. Wilmington, Del.: Scholarly Resources.

Garthoff, Raymond. *Detente and Confrontation: American-Soviet Relations from Nixon to Reagan.* Washington, D.C.: Brookings Institution, 1985.

————. *Great Transition: American-Soviet Relations and the End of the Cold War.* Washington, D.C.: Brookings Institution, 1994.

Gelb, Leslie H. "The Mind of the President." *New York Times Magazine,* October 6, 1985, 21ff.

————. "Taking Charge: The Rising Power of National Security Adviser Robert McFarlane." *New York Times Magazine,* May 26, 1985, 20ff.

George, Alexander. "The Operational Code: A Neglected Approach to the Study of Political Leaders and Decisionmaking." *International Studies Quarterly* 13 (1969): 190–222.

————. *Presidential Decisionmaking in Foreign Policy: The Effective Use of Information and Advice.* Boulder, Colo.: Westview, 1980.

————. "The Transition in U.S.-Soviet Relations, 1985–1990: An Interpretation from the Perspective of International Relations Theory and Political Psychology." *Political Psychology* 12 (1991): 409–86.

Gilbert, Dennis A. *Compendium of American Public Opinion.* New York: Facts on File Publications, 1988.

Glad, Betty. "Black-and-White Thinking: Ronald Reagan's Approach to Foreign Policy." *Political Psychology* 4 (March 1983): 33–76.

Glaser, Charles. "Why Even Good Defenses May Be Bad." *International Security* 9 (Fall 1984): 92–123.

Goldman, Kjell. *Change and Stability in Foreign Policy: The Problems and Possibilities of Détente.* Princeton: Princeton University Press, 1988.

Goleman, Daniel. *Emotional Intelligence.* New York: Bantam Books, 1995.

Greenstein, Fred I. "Ronald Reagan—Another Hidden-Hand Ike?" *P.S.: Political Science and Politics* 23 (1990): 7–13.

Griffiths, Franklyn. "Attempted Learning: Soviet Policy toward the United States in the Brezhnev Era." In *Learning in U.S. and Soviet Foreign Policy,* ed. G. W. Breslauer and P. E. Tetlock, 663–68. Boulder, Colo.: Westview, 1991.

Grunwald, Henry. "Foreign Policy under Reagan II." *Foreign Affairs* 63 (Winter 1984–1985): 219–39.

Gwertzman, Bernard. "The Shultz Method: How the New Secretary of State Is Trying to Stabilize Foreign Policy." *New York Times Magazine,* January 2, 1983, 13ff.

Haig, Alexander M., Jr. *Caveat: Realism, Reagan, and Foreign Policy.* New York: Macmillan, 1984.

Halloran, Richard. "Reagan as Commander in Chief." *New York Times Magazine,* January 15, 1984, 25ff.

Haslam, Jonathan. "Soviet Policy toward Western Europe since World War II." In *Learning in U.S. and Soviet Foreign Policy,* ed. G. W. Breslauer and P. E. Tetlock, 469–503. Boulder, Colo.: Westview, 1991.

Henkin, Louis. *Foreign Affairs and the Constitution.* New York: W. W. Norton, 1990.

Hermann, Charles F. "Changing Course: When Governments Choose to Redirect Foreign Policy." *International Studies Quarterly* 34 (1990): 3–21.

————, Charles W. Kegley Jr., and James N. Rosenau. *New Directions in the Study of Foreign Policy.* Boston: Allen and Unwin, 1987.

Hermann, Margaret G. "Personality and Foreign Policy Decision Making: A Study of 53 Heads of Government." In *Foreign Policy Decision Making,* ed. D. A. Sylvan and S. Chan. New York: Praeger, 1984.

Herr, P. M. "Consequences of Priming: Judgement and Behavior." *Journal of Personality and Social Psychology* 19 (1986): 1106–15.

————, S. J. Sherman, and R. H. Fazio. "On the Consequences of Priming: Assimilation and Contrast Effects." *Journal of Experimental Social Psychology* 19 (1983): 323–40.

Hersh, Seymour M. *The Target is Destroyed.* New York: Random House, 1986.

Higgins, E. Tory, C. P. Herman, and M. P. Zanna. *Social Cognition: The Ontario Symposium.* Hillsdale, N.J.: Lawrence Erlbaum Associates, 1981.

————, W. S. Rholes, and C. R. Jones. "Category Accessibility and Impression Formation." *Journal of Experimental Social Psychology* 13 (1977): 141–54.

Holsti, Kal J. *Why Nations Realign.* London: George Allen and Unwin, 1982.

Holsti, Ole R. "Cognitive Dynamics and Images of the Enemy." In *Image and Reality in World Politics,* ed. J. C. Farrell and A. P. Smith. New York: Columbia University Press, 1967.

————. "Foreign Policy Formation Viewed Cognitively." In *Structure of Decision,* ed. R. Axelrod. Princeton: Princeton University Press, 1976.

————. "Public Opinion and Foreign Policy: Challenges to the Almond-Lipmann Consensus." *International Studies Quarterly* 36 (1992): 439–66.

Hough, Jerry F. "The World as Viewed from Moscow." *International Journal* 37 (1982): 186–89.

Hyland, William G., ed. *The Reagan Foreign Policy.* New York: New American Library, 1987.

Iyengar, Shanto, Mark D. Peters, and Donald R. Kinder. "Experimental Demonstrations of the 'Not-So-Minimal' Consequences of Television News Programs." *American Political Science Review* 76 (1982): 848–58.

Jervis, Robert. *Perception and Misperception in International Politics.* Princeton: Princeton University Press, 1976.

————, Richard Ned Lebow, and Janice Gross Stein. *Psychology and Deterrence.* Baltimore: Johns Hopkins University Press, 1985.

Johnson, R. W. *Shootdown: The Verdict on KAL 007.* London: Chatto and Windus, 1986.

Kaufmann, William W. *A Reasonable Defense.* Washington, D.C.: Brookings Institution, 1986.

Kegley, Charles W., Jr. "How Did the Cold War Die: Principles for an Autopsy." *Mershon International Studies Review* 38 (1994): 11–42.

Kelley, Harold. "Attribution Theory in Social Psychology." In *Nebraska Symposium on Motivation,* ed. D. Levine. Vol. 2. Lincoln: University of Nebraska Press, 1967.

————. "Causal Schemata and the Attribution Process." In *Attribution: Perceiving the Causes of Behavior,* ed. E. E. Jones et al. Morristown, N.J.: General Learning Press, 1972.

Kelman, Herbert C. *International Behavior.* New York: Holt Rinehart, 1965.

Kissinger, Henry. *White House Years.* New York: Little, Brown, 1979.

Koh, Harold Hongju. *The National Security Constitution: Sharing Power after the Iran-Contra Affair.* New Haven: Yale University Press, 1990.

Koopman, Cheryl, Jack Snyder, and Robert Jervis. "American Elite Views of Relations with the Soviet Union." *Journal of Social Issues* 45 (1989): 119–38.

Larson, Deborah Welch. "Learning in U.S.-Soviet Relations: The Nixon-Kissinger Structure of Peace." In *Learning in U.S. and Soviet Foreign Policy,* ed. G. W. Breslauer and P. E. Tetlock, 350–99. Boulder, Colo.: Westview, 1991.

———. *Origins of Containment: A Psychological Approach.* Princeton: Princeton University Press, 1985.

Levy, Jack S. "Learning and Foreign Policy: Sweeping a Conceptual Minefield." *International Organization* 48 (spring 1994): 279–312.

Mandelbaum, Michael. "The Luck of the President." *Foreign Affairs: America and the World 1985* 64 (1986) 393–412.

———, and Strobe Talbott. *Reagan and Gorbachev.* New York: Council on Foreign Relations, 1987.

Mayer, Jane, and Doyle McManus. *Landslide: The Unmaking of the President, 1984–1988.* Boston: Houghton Mifflin Company, 1987.

Mayers, Teena Karsa. *Understanding Weapons and Arms Control.* Washington, D.C.: Brassey's (U.S.), 1991.

McFarlane, Robert, with Zofia Smardz. *Special Trust.* New York: Cadell and Davies, 1994.

McGuire, William J. "Attitudes and Attitude Change." In *The Handbook of Social Psychology,* ed. G. Lindzey and E. Aronson. 3d ed., vol. 2. New York: Random House, 1985.

Meese, Edwin, III. *With Reagan: The Inside Story.* Washington, D.C.: Regnery Gateway, 1992.

Mendelson, Sarah E. "Internal Battles and External Wars: Politics, Learning, and the Soviet Withdrawal from Afghanistan." *World Politics* 45 (1993): 327–60.

Menges, Constantine C. *Inside the Security Council.* New York: Simon and Schuster, 1988.

Mervin, David. *Ronald Reagan and the American Presidency.* New York: Longman, 1990.

Nincic, Miroslav. "The United States, the Soviet Union, and the Politics of Opposites." *World Politics* 40 (1988): 452–75.

Nye, Joseph S. "Gorbachev's Russia and U.S. Options." In *Gorbachev's Russia and American Foreign Policy*, ed. Seweryn Bialer and Michael Mandelbaum. Boulder, Colo.: Westview, 1988.

––––––. *The Making of America's Soviet Policy.* New York: Council on Foreign Relations, 1984.

Oberdorfer, Don. *The Turn: From Cold War to a New Era.* New York: Poseidon Press, 1991.

Page, Benjamin I., and Robert Y. Shapiro. "Effects of Public Opinion on Policy." *American Political Science Review* 77 (1983): 175–90.

––––––. "Foreign Policy and the Rational Public." *Journal of Conflict Resolution* 32 (1988): 211–47.

––––––. *The Rational Public: Fifty Years of Trends in Americans' Policy Preferences.* Chicago: University of Chicago Press, 1992.

Pfaltzgraff, Robert L., and Jacquelyn K. Davis. *National Security Decisions: The Participants Speak.* Lexington, Mass.: Lexington Books, 1990.

Pious, Richard M. "Prerogative Power and the Reagan Presidency." *Political Science Quarterly* 106 (1991): 499–510.

Powlick, Philip J. "The Attitudinal Bases for Responsiveness to Public Opinion among Foreign Policy Officials." *Journal of Conflict Resolution* 35 (1991): 611–41.

Public Papers of the Presidents: Ronald Reagan, 1981–1988. Washington, D.C.: U.S. Government Printing Office.

Quigley, Joan. *What Does Joan Say?: My Seven Years as White House Astrologer to Nancy and Ronald Reagan.* New York: Birch Lane Press, 1990.

Reagan, Ronald W. *Ronald Reagan: An American Life.* New York: Pocket Books, 1990.

––––––. *A Time for Choosing: The Speeches of Ronald Reagan, 1961–1982.* Chicago: Regnery Gateway, 1983.

––––––, with Richard G. Hubler. *My Early Life, or Where's the Rest of Me?* London: Sedgwick and Jackson, 1965.

Regan, Donald. *For the Record: From Wall Street to Washington.* New York: St. Martin's Press, 1988.

The Report of the Congressional Committees Investigating the Iran-Contra Affair: With Supplemental, Minority, and Additional Views.

U.S. House of Representatives Select Committee to Investigate Covert Arms Transactions with Iran: U.S. Senate Select Committee on Secret Military Assistance to Iran and the Nicaraguan Opposition, Washington, D.C.: U.S. Government Printing Office, 1987.

Rice, Condoleeza. "U.S.-Soviet Relations." In *Looking Back on the Reagan Presidency,* ed. Larry Berman. Baltimore: Johns Hopkins University Press, 1990.

Risse-Kappen, Thomas. "Public Opinion, Domestic Structure, and Foreign Policy in Liberal Democracies." *World Politics* 43 (1991): 479–512.

Robles, Roxana, R. Smith, C. Carver, and A. R. Wellens. "Influence of Subliminal Visual Images on the Experience of Anxiety." *Personality and Social Psychology Bulletin* 13 (1987): 399–410.

Rosati, Jerel, Joe D. Hagan, and Martin W. Sampson III. *Foreign Policy Restructuring: How Governments Respond to Global Change.* Columbia: University of South Carolina Press, 1994.

Rosenfeld, Stephen S. "Testing the Hard Line." *Foreign Affairs: America and the World 1982* 61 (1983): 489–510.

Sagan, Scott. *The Limits of Safety: Organizations, Accidents, and Nuclear Weapons.* Princeton: Princeton University Press, 1993.

Scheer, R. "Nuclear War a Real Prospect to Reagan Hard-Liners." *Chicago Sun-Times,* October 4, 1981.

Schlesinger, Arthur M., Jr. *The Imperial Presidency.* Boston: Houghton Mifflin, 1973.

Shimko, Keith L. *Images and Arms Control: Perceptions of the Soviet Union in the Reagan Administration.* Ann Arbor: University of Michigan Press, 1991.

———. "Reagan on the Soviet Union and the Nature of International Conflict." *Political Psychology* 13 (1992): 353–78.

Shoemaker, Christopher C. *The NSC Staff: Counseling the Council.* Boulder, Colo.: Westview, 1991.

Shultz, George P. "New Realities and New Ways of Thinking." *Foreign Affairs* 63 (1985): 705–21.

———. *Turmoil and Triumph: My Years as Secretary of State.* New York: Charles Scribner's Sons, 1993.

Sigelman, Lee, and Carol K. Sigelman. "The Politics of Popular Culture: Campaign Cynicism and 'The Candidate.'" *Sociology and Social Research* 58 (1974): 272–77.

Silverstein, Brett. "Enemy Images: The Psychology of U.S. Attitudes and Cognitions Regarding the Soviet Union." *American Psychologist* 44 (June 1989) 903–913.

———, and Catherine Flamenbaum. "Biases in the Perception and Cognition of the Actions of Enemies." *Journal of Social Issues* 45 (1989): 51–72.

Smith, Hedrick. *The Power Game.* New York: Random House, 1988.

Smith, Jean Edward. *The Constitution and American Foreign Policy.* St. Paul, Minn.: West, 1989.

Snyder, Mark, Elizabeth D. Tanke, and Ellen Berscheid. "Social Perception and Interpersonal Behavior: On the Self-Fulfilling Nature of Social Stereotypes." *Journal of Personality and Social Psychology* 35 (1977): 656–66.

Spanier, John. *American Foreign Policy since World War II.* Washington, D.C.: Congressional Quarterly Press, 1991.

Stein, Janice Gross. "Cognitive Psychology and Political Learning: Gorbachev as an Uncommitted Thinker and Motivated Learner." In *International Relations Theory and the Transformation of the International System,* ed. R. N. Lebow and T. Risse-Kappen. New York: Columbia University Press, 1995.

———. "Ideas, Even Good Ideas, Are Not Enough: Changing Canada's Foreign and Defense Policies." *International Journal* 50 (winter 1994–1995): 40–70.

Stuart, D., and H. Starr. "The 'Inherent Bad Faith Model' Reconsidered: Dulles, Kennedy, and Kissinger," *Political Psychology* 3 (1981–1982): 1–33.

Talbott, Strobe. *Deadly Gambits: The Reagan Administration and the Stalemate in Nuclear Arms Control.* New York: Alfred A. Knopf, 1984.

———. *The Russians and Reagan.* New York: Council on Foreign Relations, 1984.

Tetlock, Philip E. "Learning in U.S. and Soviet Foreign Policy: In Search of an Elusive Concept." In *Learning in U.S. and Soviet*

Foreign Policy, ed. G. W. Breslauer and P. E. Tetlock, 20–61. Boulder, Colo.: Westview, 1991.

Thies, Wallace J. "Learning in U.S. Policy toward Europe." In *Learning in U.S. and Soviet Foreign Policy,* ed. G. W. Breslauer and P. E. Tetlock, 158–207. Boulder, Colo.: Westview, 1991.

Tower, John, Edmund Muskie, and Brent Scowcroft. *The Tower Commission Report: The Full Text of the President's Special Review Board.* New York: Bantam Books, 1987.

Tucker, Robert W. "Toward a New Détente." *New York Times Magazine,* December 9, 1984.

Turner, Michael. "Foreign Policy and the Reagan Administration." In *Reagan's First Four Years,* by J. D. Lees and M. Turner. Manchester: Manchester University Press, 1988.

———. "The Reagan White House, the Cabinet, and the Bureaucracy." In *Reagan's First Four Years,* by J. D. Lees and M. Turner. Manchester: Manchester University Press, 1988.

Tversky, Amos, and Daniel Kahneman. "Availability: A Heuristic for Judging Frequency and Probability." *Cognitive Psychology* 5 (1973): 207–32.

Vertzberger, Yaacov I. *The World in Their Minds: Information Processing, Cognition, and Perception in Foreign Policy Decision Making.* Stanford: Stanford University Press, 1990.

Waldstein, Frederic A. "Cabinet Government: The Reagan Management Model." In *The Reagan Years,* ed. Joseph Hogan. Manchester: Manchester University Press, 1990.

Waltz, Kenneth N. *Theory of International Politics.* New York: McGraw-Hill, 1979.

Weber, Renee, and Jennifer Crocker. "Cognitive Processes in the Revision of Stereotypic Beliefs." *Journal of Personality and Social Psychology* 45 (1983): 961–77.

Weber, Steven. "Interactive Learning in U.S.-Soviet Arms Control." In *Learning in U.S. and Soviet Foreign Policy,* ed. G. W. Breslauer and P. E. Tetlock, 784–824. Boulder, Colo.: Westview, 1991.

Weekly Compilation of Presidential Documents [WCPD], 1981–1988. Washington, D.C.: U.S. Government Printing Office.

Weinberger, Caspar W. *Fighting for Peace: Seven Critical Years in the Pentagon.* New York: Warner Books, 1983.

Weisman, Steven R. "The Influence of William Clark." *New York Times Magazine,* August 14, 1983, 17ff.

White, Ralph K. "Empathizing with the Rulers of the USSR." *Political Psychology* 4 (1983): 121–37.

Wills, Gary. *Reagan's America: Innocents at Home.* Garden City, N.Y.: Doubleday, 1987.

Woodward, Bob. *Veil: The Secret Wars of the CIA.* New York: Simon and Schuster, 1987.

Yankelovich, Daniel, and John Doble. "The Public Mood." *Foreign Affairs* 63 (Fall 1984): 33–46.

Yankelovich, Daniel, and Richard Smoke. "America's 'New Thinking.'" *Foreign Affairs* 67 (1988): 1–17.

Zimmerman, Karsten. "Decision in March: The Genesis of the 'Star Wars' Speech." In *The Reagan Administration: A Reconstruction of Strength?,* ed. Helga Haftendorn and Jakob Schissler. New York: Walter de Gruyter, 1988.

Index